Dearest Eleanor

Thank you s[...]

helping us to [...]

Much love + grat[...]

Letty & Anita

x x x

C000132238

Anita Gilbert and Letty Butler (aka Bert & Butler) have been friends and colleagues for over twenty years, and between them have over forty years' experience in the business.

Letty is a jobbing actor and comedienne, with extensive credits for stage and screen, and is represented by United Agents. She's also a professional creative coach (Distinction from Kingstown College/EMCC accredited), with three degrees (BA Hons 2:1 in English Literature and Theatre Studies from Leeds University, BA Honours 2:1 in Acting from LAMDA, and an MA Distinction in Creative Writing from Sheffield Hallam University). For her writing, Letty has won the SHU Creative Writing Award, the OTS Novel Slam and the Cranked Anvil Short Story Prize. She's also been shortlisted for the Bridport Prize, a Northern Writers' Award, Bath Flash Fiction and Mslexia.

Anita is also from an acting background and worked professionally after graduating from ALRA in 1996. From the late '90s to 2015, Anita worked alongside Philippa Howell (PHPM) as an assistant agent. Together they built a thriving theatrical agency, representing 150 clients. Anita holds an MA (Distinction) in Professional Voice Practice from Royal Birmingham Conservatoire, and now works as a professional voice and accent practitioner, prepping actors on a daily basis either one to one, or as part of the rehearsal process in theatre, TV, and film, through her business Speakeasy Voice and Accent Coaching. Anita is currently a Senior Lecturer at Leeds Conservatoire and is represented as a creative by Nicola Bolton Management.

LETTY BUTLER & ANITA GILBERT

The Jobbing Actor

A COACHING PROGRAMME FOR ACTORS

BECAUSE RESTING IS HARDER THAN IT SOUNDS

NICK HERN BOOKS
LONDON
WWW.NICKHERNBOOKS.CO.UK

A Nick Hern Book

The Jobbing Actor first published in Great Britain in 2023
by Nick Hern Books Limited, The Glasshouse, 49a Goldhawk Road,
London W12 8QP

Copyright © 2023 Letty Butler and Anita Gilbert
Illustrations © 2023 Letty Butler

Letty Butler and Anita Gilbert have asserted their moral right to be identified
as the authors of this work

Designed and typeset by Alan Frost

Printed and bound in Great Britain by Mimeo Ltd, Huntingdon,
Cambridgeshire PE29 6XX

A CIP catalogue record for this book is available from the British Library

ISBN 978 1 83904 085 6

CONTENTS

WARNING

CONTAINS EVERYTHING YOU NEED TO SURVIVE
AND THRIVE AS A JOBBING ACTOR!

FOREWORD

Hello and Welcome!

We are Bert & Butler, the co-founders of *The Jobbing Actor*. Before we crack on, we thought we'd better explain who we are, why we're doing this and what 'it' is exactly.

What Is It Then?

The Jobbing Actor is an innovative six-week coaching programme designed *specifically* for actors, by actors and accredited coaches. It's not just another 'how to' guide, telling you what you already know, but a professional self-development programme that's high on impact, low on bullshit.

Over the course of six weeks, we will guide you through a combination of industry-focused and holistic exercises and challenges. This will enable you to take an objective view of where you're at personally and professionally. By offering structure and support to hit self-defined targets and reach overarching goals across a specified timeline, *The Jobbing Actor* aims to empower every actor to reclaim ownership of their career. You included.

Each week homes in on a key element of the business – skills; networking; branding; resting; rejection and diversifying. You are held accountable to your own targets through guided reflexive practice, which is more fun than it sounds. By the end of the six-week programme you will have a fully fledged journalling habit in addition to a wealth of tools and techniques designed to maintain the resilience and motivation you need to pursue your career ambitions in a positive, mental-health-friendly way. These toolkits are sustainable. We're equipping you for life.

We know that actors are creative beings, which is why we've designed the programme to be as inspiring and uplifting as it is empowering and effective. *The Jobbing Actor* is designed to be a powerful, creative and energising experience that will enable you to carry on doing what you love.

This isn't just a book. It's a mindset. Because resting doesn't have to be dull. It can actually be a powerful creative catalyst to propel you towards success.

Who Needs a Coach?

Here at Bert & Butler HQ, we believe that *everyone* should have a coach, especially if they're interested in being better at what they do.

But Why?

When you go it alone, both personally and professionally, you often fail to recognise the issues that stand in your way, or if you do, you don't necessarily know how to fix them. The result is that somewhere along the line, you stop improving. Humans are happiest when they're learning, growing and striving for meaningful goals. So when we plateau, even subconsciously, it impacts our happiness.

Coaches are your external eyes and ears, providing a more accurate picture of your reality. They enable you to recognise the fundamentals, break your actions down and then help you build them back up again. We tend to think that coaches are just for those in the world of sport, but why? If top athletes have room for improvement and yield results from external support, imagine how much impact a coach could have on you in your field of expertise.

> *'It's not just how good you are now, it's how good you're going to be that matters.'*
>
> Atul Gawande – American surgeon, writer and public health researcher

We know that coaching can be an expensive business, and that not everyone's in a position to fork out for one-to-one sessions, so here we are – ready to help you reveal the rust, whip out the polish and make you shine.

Who Are We?

Between us we have over forty years' worth of experience in the business. We've hit it from pretty much every angle imaginable. Bert trained as an actress (ALRA) and spent ten years working, before jumping ship to become an agent. She then hot-footed it to the Royal Birmingham Conservatoire where she got an MA Distinction in Professional Voice Practice. Bert is currently a Senior Voice Lecturer at Leeds Conservatoire, coaches actors on a one-to-one basis and offers voice and accent production support across the UK theatre and film industry.*

Butler trained at LAMDA in 2009 and has directed, produced, written and acted for stage and screen ever since. She also has a BA Hons in English Literature and Theatre Studies from Leeds University and an MA Distinction in Creative Writing from SHU because she bloody loves education. Butler is a qualified coach with a Distinction from Kingstown College and currently coaches creatives across a range of genres, but primarily actors and writers.** She's still very much a jobbing actress, and therefore with you on the frontline and fully aware of just how challenging it is.

Why Are We Doing This?

We're big fans of not beating around the bush, so here are some nice bullet points for you:

- The point of all the above is that we *know* what it means to be an actor – how utterly exhilarating and rewarding it is, but also how hard, lonely and demoralising it can be. When we realised we had the combined knowledge and skillsets to help with the latter, we decided to do something about it.

- The current stats regarding actors' mental health and wellbeing are shocking. Suicide rates are soaring. You only need to spend a second on Twitter to witness it first-hand with the multiple cries for help from struggling actors. In writing this book, we're aiming to contribute to the wider conversation in the hope that it will have a positive impact on these frightening figures.

---

* For more info on Bert's voice and accent coaching, head to her website: www.speakeasyvoice.co.uk
** For coaching enquiries with Butler, head to her website: www.lettybutler.com

- One-off masterclasses or Q&As are a great way to connect with industry professionals, practise networking and find inspiration, but can sometimes exacerbate feelings of despondency and failure if nothing comes of it; for instance, if the casting director doesn't immediately bring you in or the agent doesn't sign you. We want to offer something that isn't dependent on anyone else, something that is truly yours, and that no one can take away from you. Which ties in rather nicely with…

- Sustainability! We want to offer you something that lasts longer than one or two hours, something with longevity, something for life – which is why our programme is sustainable. You can use these tools and techniques to support your career *forever*.

- This is the book we wanted when we left drama school, when we had our first massive rejection, when we couldn't find an agent and when we were in a seemingly interminable period of rest. This is the book that didn't exist when we needed it most. Now it does.

Who Is It For?

As the title suggests, this book is aimed primarily at actors (at any stage of their career) but that's not to say it's exclusively for actors. And let's be honest, it's very rare to find an actor whose sole job is acting anyway. You may be a writer, filmmaker, artist, photographer, designer, etc., as well as an actor. You may not be an actor at all! That's completely fine. We believe that this book will enable any creative being to implement positive and long-lasting change, whatever their craft.

So without further ado, we give you, *The Jobbing Actor*!

INTRODUCTION

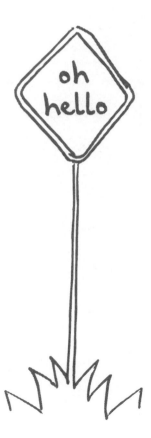

How Does It Work?

As we've established, *The Jobbing Actor* is a six-week coaching programme designed specifically for actors. It's based on the leading research around behavioural change, which indicates that self-awareness and reflection plus minor habit change can lead to major results. Each week builds on the last and we recommend you do it in order to fully harness the benefits of the programme and instigate long-term behavioural change.

If you're the kind of person who hates reading instructions, we get it. We hate them too. So we've tried to make this section as short and painless as possible. If you're still tempted to bypass it, ask yourself this question:

'Do I want this to work?'

If the answer if 'yes' – excellent! Read on. If you aren't sure – well, you're here now, so you might as well give it a whirl.

Let's crack on, shall we?

The Preparation Station

Before we hit you (gently) with Week One, we're going to take you through The Preparation Station. Think of it as a sort of mental MOT to ensure your engine's up to the journey ahead. We recommend spending a couple of hours in this section, preferably when you're feeling particularly fired up about the prospect of the career-enhancing adventure ahead. First up, we're going to introduce you to some key terms you'll come across as you motor through the programme.

Vroom.

Weekly Themes

At the beginning of every week, we introduce an overall theme with an accompanying practical exercise. The theme is directly related to the industry – for example, personal branding or networking.

Midweek Motivation

You'll find a Midweek Motivation halfway through each week to give you a little boost. These are quick, practical exercises that support the weekly theme and offer a timely shove in the right direction when motivation is prone to waning. Some exercises are industry-centric but others are more holistic – such as The Wellness Toolkit or The Relationship Inventory. Why? Because this process is designed to help you explore the relationship with yourself as well as your career.

'I think one of the most important lessons I've learnt is to define my own success and set achievable goals under my control.'

Orion Lee – Oscar-nominated actor

Targets and Goals

What's the difference? Stunning question!

A goal is an overarching ambition. Something meaty. Something big. Probably something vaguely overwhelming.

A target is a stepping stone towards that goal.

We'll get you setting goals in The Preparation Station and targets on a daily basis. It's basically that whole 'take care of the pennies and the pounds will take care of themselves' mentality. If you consistently complete targets, they soon add up to goals.

We encourage you to create goals and targets in two key areas: Career, and Health and Wellness. YOU are your tool, which is why we put equal emphasis on both areas. In the words of Mr Chekhov *'If you want to work on your art, you must first work on yourself'*.

Treats

When instigating change, it's important to reward ourselves when we do hit targets, otherwise we run the risk of feeling like life is all schlep and no sizzle. Be playful with your treats. Take some time to make a list of all the things you genuinely enjoy, or perhaps used to enjoy but now deny yourself – either through lack of time, money or energy. We've created a special space for you to do just this on page 30.

Treats don't have to be bank-breaking. We're big fans of sticker charts, despite the fact we're not four years old. Simple rewards create simple pleasure. Think small but mighty.

Trip-ups

In the goal-setting section, there's a space called 'Trip-ups'. This gives you a chance to think about and record potential obstacles that could get in the way of you hitting your targets. They may be people, situations, habits or thought patterns. It's useful to keep reviewing these throughout the process, so you can learn from your trip-ups and be better equipped to handle them in the future. It all comes back to generating awareness; one of the core factors of creating lasting behavioural change.

Daily Reflections

At the end of each day, we encourage you to reflect in your journal. But why?

Reflective practice reduces stress and enhances self-awareness, self-esteem and sleep, as well as boosting emotional intelligence, positivity and problem-solving abilities. Through journalling, we learn to develop a greater understanding of ourselves and others. It can also boost our creative thinking and supports active engagement in our work – what's not to like?

The writing! We hear you cry. Look, the action of writing down a specific event or thought, in your journal, makes it tangible. You can see it. It's making a pact with yourself to deal with it and not push thoughts/plans/ideas/feelings to the back of your mind. In return, you'll get calm and clarity, instead of a 2 a.m., insomnia-inducing thought-party.

> *'We do not learn from experience... we learn from reflecting on experience.'*
>
> John Dewey – American philosopher

How Do I Do It?

You begin by filling out your overarching goals for the week in the following categories: Career, Health and Wellness, and Treats. The second stage is to…

Map Your Week

Once you've completed the initial practical exercise at the start of each week, it's time to set your targets for the next six days – a process we refer to as Mapping Your Week. This is best done on a Sunday night or Monday morning, so you're all set for the week ahead. It's crucial to have access to your diary so you can be realistic about what you can actually achieve that week. Work out exactly when you can do what and diarise it – then fully commit to it. If we carve out a chunk of time to complete a specific task and/or write it on a to-do list, we are far more likely to actually do it. Plus it relieves stress and offers structure amidst the chaos.

As you're setting your targets, make sure you channel the weekly theme so that you're incorporating and cementing new knowledge regularly throughout the process.

We appreciate that it won't always go to plan because life's not like that. Especially if you're an actor. But setting intentions is crucial to bringing meaning and purpose, so it's better to have a plan and deviate from it, than float about hoping something marvellous will happen.

> *'In preparing for battle I have always found that plans are useless, but planning is indispensable.'*
>
> Dwight D. Eisenhower – 34th President of the United States of America

Day to Day

You start each day by writing down your daily target, so it's in the forefront of your mind. Remember, a target can be tiny!

At the end of every day, it's time to reflect. We invite you to let it all out and describe the day in all its gory or glorious detail, then pinpoint one positive thing that happened. By harnessing the habit of looking for the positives, you are actually rewiring your brain into a happier, more productive mind-set. And it's not some happy-clappy nonsense, it's all backed up by scientific research in the realms of neuroplasticity. Every single time you focus on something you are grateful for, you give yourself a shot of serotonin and dopamine. The more we activate these gratitude circuits in our brain, the stronger our capacity for productivity and positivity. Hoopla!

Once the daily reflection is out of the way, you focus specifically on your goal progress. Are you on track? Do you want to add any more targets to the week? Can you identify anything that curbed your progress? Do you need to give yourself a pat on the back or a kick up the arse?

Things to consider when reflecting:

* Are there signs that show you when, where and how best you achieve your targets?

* Are there patterns that shed light on when/why you don't complete a task?

These sections are really useful to look back on when you're setting targets for the following week. You'll be able to analyse your behaviours more effectively and make plans to accommodate or combat them as you move forward.

A Note About Being Mean

If you don't hit your targets, don't beat yourself up – learn from it. Analyse where, when and how you went wrong so you can overcome those obstacles next time. If you skip a day here and there – so what? It doesn't matter. This is your programme, your process and you're the one calling the shots. Make it work for you. However, we do wish to emphasise that it is the regular engagement that will embed the behavioural change we keep banging on about.

Any Other Business?

Yes, actually, but only a tiny bit.

The Inspiration Station

We've invented this section to plant seeds in your creative brain. You'll find a few suggestions to help you start planning targets and treats, and encourage your brain to start focusing on these areas. It's basically a catalyst for the subconscious – once you trigger new ideas, your brain starts finding more and has a secret party on its own when you're asleep or thinking about something completely different, like ferrets or who's going to win *Bake Off*.

Sample Journal Pages

Over the following pages, you'll find a sample week which will give you an insight into how the programme is set out and what your journalling might look like. Use it as inspiration for your own musings, but remember, it's not a fixed blueprint. Take what works for you and kick the rest to the curb.

Additional Templates

We know that everyone will have a slightly different approach to this process. For example, you may love the journal pages and exercises but be reluctant to write directly in this book. Or perhaps you want to add elements of the programme to an existing journalling habit? Perhaps you have a professional system in place but want to embellish it with elements of ours? And that's all marvellous! We salute you in all your unique glory.

To ensure we're catering for everyone, we've made our key templates, exercises and additional journal pages available for downloading and printing. So, if you want to go off-piste and do things your way, head to www.nickhernbooks.co.uk/jobbing-actor-templates where you'll find an array of downloadable documents designed to suit you.

AT THE BEGINNING OF EVERY <u>WEEK</u>
YOU'LL GET PAGES THAT LOOK LIKE THIS...

WELCOME TO A NEW WEEK!

Week Number: **1**   **Date w/c:**...........................

———————— THIS WEEK'S GOALS ————————

Career

....
....
....
....

Health and Wellness

....
....
....
....

Treats

....
....
....
....

Why are the above goals important to me?

....
....
....
....

What trip-ups might prevent me from hitting my goals?

....
....
....
....

Monday

....
....
....

Tuesday

....
....
....

Wednesday

....
....
....

Thursday

....
....
....

Friday

....
....
....

Saturday

....
....
....

Sunday

....
....
....

WHICH MAY LOOK SOMETHING LIKE THIS
ONCE YOU'VE FILLED THEM IN...

WELCOME TO A NEW WEEK!

Week Number: **1**   **Date w/c:** *27th November*

THIS WEEK'S GOALS

Career

Update Spotlight page
Work on my General American accent

Health and Wellness

Sit somewhere peaceful every day for 10 mins
Try that new kickboxing class Gary keeps banging on about

Treats

Do a fun activity – tickets to a gig/match/cinema?
Invite Tariq + Daisy round for dinner

Why are the above goals important to me?

I know my Gen. Am. accent isn't up to scratch and lets me down in auditions. I want to feel confident in the room and ready to go at the drop of a hat. I haven't seen Tariq and Daisy for ages, and need to do some bonding. Plus we always have a great time.

What trip-ups might prevent me from hitting my goals?

- Being hungover
- Being disorganised
- Overloading my social calendar
- Procrastination/social media

Monday

Research accent tools online/apps

Tuesday

Update Spotlight page (afternoon)

Wednesday

Text Tariq and Daisy to arrange dinner
Email Gary for kickboxing class details

Thursday

Gig/match/cinema

Friday

30 min accent work at 11am

Saturday

Tariq and Daisy for dinner?

Sunday

Day off

**AND EVERY <u>DAY</u> YOU'LL GET A PAGE THAT
LOOKS LIKE THIS...**

DAY 1 MONDAY

'Quote of the day.'

—

Day/Date: ....

Daily Target: ....

How did today go?

....
....
....
....
....
....
....

What was one good thing that happened today?

....
....
....
....

--------------------- **TARGET PROGRESS** ---------------------

Did I complete any targets?

....

Did I identify any trip-ups?

....

Any additional targets?

....

WHICH MAY LOOK END UP LOOKING SOMETHING LIKE THIS...

DAY 1 MONDAY

> *'If all the circumstances of acting are made too easy,*
> *then there's no grain of sand to make the pearl.'*
>
> Peter Sarsgaard – American actor

—

Day/Date: *Monday 27th November*

Daily Target: *Research accent tools online/apps*

How did today go?

Weirdly stressful day. Overslept so I missed my peaceful 10 mins in garden. – think it set me off on wrong foot. Nightmare shift at work. Still no news re audition. Think it must have 'gone another way'. AGAIN. I don't know why they can't just tell you, I mean, it's not that hard to send an email, is it? Bloody rude. In other news, I think I've broken a tooth. Yawn. On the plus side, decided against beer tonight so might have one at gig tomorrow. Or just go for 5 booze-free days. Definitely feel much more 'on it' when I don't drink. Going to set alarm half an hour earlier tomo so I don't miss my quiet garden time.

What was one good thing that happened today?

Managed to find a free accent app that's v.easy to use. It has bitesize sessions, so I can keep polishing it up as I'm on the move. Game-changer! Going to try and get into the habit of doing 10 mins a day. Might work my way across the globe.

—

TARGET PROGRESS

—

Did I complete any targets?

Yep. Accent research. Plus Gary got in touch + has booked me a free trial for kickboxing on Sat morn.

Did I identify any trip-ups?

Oversleeping. Change to a louder alarm tone!

Any additional targets?

Get tooth fixed.

THE PREPARATION
AND INSPIRATION STATIONS

Goal-setting

Goals provide you with focus and purpose and help to eliminate time-wasting. They also nurture self-esteem, discipline, tenacity and resolve. Yes please!

There's an art to goal-setting. Everyone has their own ways of instigating change but here's one of our favourite techniques. It's twofold. We suggest you do both parts before starting Week One.

Part One: Find Your Whys

Quite simply ask yourself: What do I want and *why* do I want it?

Whenever we set goals in life, they have to relate to reasons, because *reasons drive behaviour*. If we don't fully comprehend what we want to get out of achieving a goal, we are less likely to see it through.

For example, it's no good saying 'I want to get fit.' You need to follow it up with the reason why – 'I want to get fit so I have the energy and confidence to deliver in the audition room.'

Motivation tends to wane if we don't see immediate results, which is why it's important to make a list of all your reasons right at the beginning while they're still fresh. Not only does the very act of writing embed them in your subconscious, it also helps to have them somewhere to hand, so whenever you need a bit of a motivational boost along the way, you know exactly where to look.

'Tell me, what is it you plan to do with your one wild and precious life?'
Mary Oliver – writer

So, without further ado, grab a pen, find a quiet spot and really think about why you are going through this process. Go deep and get honest with yourself. It may surprise you.

Here are some prompts to get the cogs turning:

- Why am I here?
- What has bought me to this point?
- What would I like to get out of this process?
- What will life look like if I achieve this goal?

Here are some examples of what you might write:

- I want to make the most of my 'resting' time.
- I want to broaden my skillset so I am more castable.
- I'd like to establish a daily routine.
- I'd like to put some structure into my days so I feel more in control.
- I want to feel more positive about my career.

Try and use this technique whenever you're goal-setting in future. And if you can *visualise* success, you're far more likely to succeed. Historically, visualisation was dismissed as 'woo-woo' but is now a popular and respected technique used by everyone from world class athletes to leading CEOs.

But What Is It?

Simply put, visualisation is a brain-training technique. More specifically, it's the practice of imagining getting the things you want out of life in order to make them happen. It involves using all of the senses to really envision and experience what success would feel like.

Visualisation works by activating your creative subconscious which then generates the motivation and ideas required to help you reach your goals. It also enables us to recognise and subsequently attract the resources, people and conditions we need in order succeed, in accordance with the law of attraction. In scientific terms, you're actively reprogramming your neural pathways by imagining success. And bizarrely, the brain doesn't actually know the difference. So if you imagine a desired future state in full sensory detail, your brain's neuro-imagery records the future state as if it's true today. Therefore, you subconsciously create opportunities and pathways to get to that place.

> *'Whatever you move towards, moves towards you.'*
> Jim Rohn – entrepreneur, author and motivational speaker

How Do I Do It?

- Find a quiet spot.

- Take five deep breaths, in through the nose, out through the mouth.

- Set a timer for five minutes.

- Imagine what you want in detail, engaging all five senses.

- Really connect with your emotions. How does it feel to accomplish this goal.

- Do this until the timer pings.

Ideally you'd do this twice a day – once in the morning and once before bed. Some people like to write down their desired outcome (in the present tense – as if it's already happened/happening) on an index card or create vision boards as physical reminders.

There's tons of different visualisation techniques, so get googling, see what's out there and find what works for you.

Part Two: Setting Your Goals

Why be SMART when you could just SIT down?!

There's a much-loved and widely used acronym for goal-setting which is SMART.

This encourages you to create goals that are Specific, Measurable, Achievable, Realistic and Time-sensitive. But we've got a little bit of an issue with it...

The 'A' and 'R' stand for 'achievable and realistic' which are basically the same thing in our book. And why would you limit yourself from the off? Why go for something 'achievable' or 'realistic' when you could go for something truly life-changing and inspiring? This is no place for glass ceilings!

It's also worth mentioning that in some interpretations, the 'R' stands for 'Relevant'. We don't like this much either – why would anyone create an irrelevant goal?! It's also a bit confusing to use an acronym with two possible meanings, so we've gone off-piste and created our own. We think it's simpler, easier to remember, more fun and more effective.

SIT! (that's our acronym, not an instruction)

Once you've got clarity around why you would like to create change, it's an excellent idea to ensure you create goals you can SIT with. What does that mean? It means your goals need to be:

Specific, Inspiring and Time-sensitive

When you're setting goals now or in the future, check in with each of the following categories and make sure you're sitting all over them. (Sorry.)

- Specific – *What exactly?*

What *exactly* do you want? Be as detailed as possible. For example: 'I want to work on my craft' pales in comparison to 'I want to improve my audition technique by finding a relevant workshop'.

A crucial question to ask yourself at this point is: *How will I know when I've achieved my goal?*

This is easy to answer when you're focusing on something straightforward and simple to gauge, like losing weight or running a 10k. It is slightly trickier if the goal is less tangible, such as 'I want to improve my relationship with my agent', or 'I want to build my confidence.'

If your goal falls into the less tangible category, we recommend setting up ways of monitoring your progress, for example, diarising weekly reviews that encourage you to consider powerful questions such as: *What's working well? What have I learned? How can I implement it moving forwards?* This will enable you to constantly track your progress, and keep your mind focused on the task in hand.

● Inspiring – *Got goosebumps?*

If you're not truly-madly-deeply inspired by your goals, chances are you're not going to show up for them. This is a really good place for a visualisation or three. Take the opportunity to really imagine what achieving this goal would feel like and how it would impact your life. Wallow in the glory until you get goosebumps on your knees. No goosebumps = not the right goal.

● Time-sensitive – *By when?*

Making sure your goals are time-sensitive is crucial to success. This means giving yourself challenging but realistic deadlines. When we are mindfully time-bound, we generally achieve more than we ever thought possible. The forthcoming exam, submission window or job interview – can propel us into powerful action. So...

Confirm your deadline and COMMIT to it

We know this can feel overwhelming, which is why you need a tactical time-frame. Can you break down your big dream into smaller achievable daily, weekly and monthly targets? It is this process that alleviates a feeling of being overwhelmed and makes your goals attainable. This process will also force a healthy dose of clarity on what's really required to make this dream a reality.

'A goal without a plan is just a wish.'
Antoine de Saint-Exupery – French writer and pioneering aviator

—

The Inspiration Station

Below are some suggestions to ignite your imagination when goal-setting. We've put them into categories, but don't feel bound by these. Life is fluid and difficult to compartmentalise, so some targets might be applicable to more than one category. Don't worry about this for a second.

Career

● Create a Self-Tape Team via WhatsApp – a group of fellow actors who help each other out when an audition lands. A supportive team is great for practising if auditions are thin on the ground and you want to keep each other inspired and motivated.

● Check/update your Spotlight CV (sounds obvious but when was the last time you actually did this?)

● Make a list of all the films/TV shows you like with names of casting directors, directors and producers. (This will come in handy when we get to the Networking section!)

● Brush up a skill on your CV that is a bit rusty (accents, trumpet-playing, snooker, etc.) – or learn a new one.

● Set up a playgroup. No, we're not talking toddlers. We're talking about starting a play-sharing group with fellow actors in which to exchange scripts and plays, and perhaps even read them aloud.

Health and Wellness

● Perform a random act of kindness. Why? Compassion releases happiness chemicals in your brain (dopamine, serotonin, oxytocin and endorphins) which make you feel good! You'll find a whole host of ideas on page 90.

● Rediscover the familiar – go for a walk in your local area, but choose roads you've never taken before and see where they take you.

● Download a podcast you've never listened to before and treat yourself to half an hour of stimulating newness.

● Switch off from social media for the day. If you can't manage a whole day, start with one hour and build from there.

● Whack on your favourite playlist and dance like a demon for ten minutes. You will not believe how fun it is.

Treats

- Buy yourself something that makes you happy. A new book?
  The latest gadget? Fresh tulips?

- Go to a free museum or gallery or gig.

- Plan something to look forward to – it could be a hike with friends,
  a trip to the flicks or even a new activity you've always fancied having
  a bash at. Anyone for zorbing?!

- Binge a box set or watch a favourite film you haven't seen for years.

- Hop on a train and visit a new town/city/village in the surrounding area
  – make it an adventure and take a friend or family member.

- Treat yourself to something truly delicious. You may want to spend the
  day researching recipes and cooking something extravagant for family
  or friends. Or you might prefer to gobble a 99 flake on a park bench.
  Whatever gets the tastebuds tingling is fine by us!

Over to you!

THE PROGRAMME

HOLD ON A TICKET!

How are you going to reward yourself when you've completed this process?

This needs to be something epic, something that will keep you tethered when your motivation is having a weekend away in Margate. This is beyond 'treat' territory. It's something you REALLY BLOODY WANT (within the realms of your control, obvs). Write it down now and keep visualising it happening as you work your way through the programme. You could even make a poster-sized version and stick it somewhere visible to keep you focused.

My Epic Reward is…

....

....

....

....

....

....

....

....

....

....

Very good. Sounds great.

WEEK
TOOLKIT

Week One: Toolkit

Actors spend their lives waiting. Waiting to audition. Waiting to hear the outcome. Waiting for someone to grant them the opportunity to be an actor.

Er, WRONG!

If you do something every single day that makes you an actor, you *are* an actor.

You're always an actor whether you're working or not, but it's up to you to make sure you are always *ready* to work. YOU ARE YOUR BUSINESS. It's as simple as that. You have to make sure every part of your business is in good working order at all times – your voice, your body, your brain and your 'toolkit' (i.e. your skillset).

> *'90% of this job is not acting, but making sure you are ready for it.'*
> Paapa Essiedu – actor

This first week of the programme is all about how to maintain a constant state of readiness by paying particular attention to your toolkit. There is nothing worse than feeling unprepared when a last-minute, potentially life-changing audition comes in. Putting a little time, effort and yes – occasionally money – aside to build on or refresh your skills is essential (not to mention tax deductible). The readier you are, the more confident you will feel in the room. The more skills you have, the more findable you are in a Spotlight search and ultimately, the more chance you have of landing a job. It's simple maths.

If a part requires horse-riding and you haven't so much as sat on a donkey, you're not going to get seen for it. It's equally futile to have a chokka-block toolkit full of rusty spanners. Going to an audition claiming you're fluent in Urdu when you haven't spoken it for twelve years is only going to result in embarrassment – not just for you, but the casting director who's suggested you. Do you think they'll ever bring you in again? No. You wouldn't employ a plumber who once showed up with a banana to fix the shower would you?

But we get it. As a performer, you're most likely juggling resting jobs whilst waiting for that audition, or perhaps you're in the midst of a tough theatre tour with scant spare time to learn how to skateboard. But in the words of Coldplay, 'nobody said it was easy'. The two biggest factors in creating change are persistence and effort, in addition to tiny habits and a growth mindset. The trick is to start small and believe you can do it. We're not asking you to sign up to do a ten-week intensive clowning course, just ten minutes of focused work on acquiring or maintaining a skill every day can make all the difference.

> *'Small habits don't add up, they compound. Tiny changes.*
> *Remarkable results.'*
>
> James Clear – author of *Atomic Habits*

An Exercise: Skills ETC

Get a piece of paper, some pens and give yourself at least half an hour for this exercise. Make three columns: Existing, Tactical and Curious (ETC).

Existing

What skills have you already got? List them *all*. Languages, sports, instruments – even weird and wacky things you might not deem relevant. You never know what a job might require.

Underline the ones that need work and put a star next to any that you are already skilled at.

Tactical

List any skills that might enhance your professional appeal. Accents? Audio narration? Motion capture?

If you need inspiration, think about people in your life and all the things they can do. We tend to forget that characters are based on real people, with real skills. Yes, you might be required to whip out some stage combat or historical dance for a theatre audition, but what about commercials, TV and films? It's more likely you'll be reading for a character who can play golf, ride a motorbike or shuffle a deck of cards, so look at contemporary, everyday skills *in addition* to traditional 'drama school skills'.

Once you've done that, think about films, TV series or plays you've watched and what was required of the actors in them. A specific accent? Underwater swimming? Pancake tossing? Doesn't matter how irrelevant it seems, get it down.

Curious

Make a third list of activities or things that interest you. Dig deep.

If you've always harboured a deep fascination with taxidermy or skydiving or becoming a croupier, get it on the list. We can't emphasise enough that you *never know what casting directors or producers are looking for*, so nothing's ever wasted. Plus, if you enjoy learning something, the likelihood is that you'll put the work in to achieve it and you'll always have something interesting to talk about in the audition.

Pick one skill to focus from any of the three lists and incorporate it into your targets this week. Remember to start small. Tiny habits = big changes.

Keep this list somewhere safe. Next time you find yourself 'waiting', decide that you're going to use the time proactively instead and tackle your toolkit. It's not waiting, it's development.

'Having had two careers I am constantly amazed at how many skills can cross over from one career to another. When you find yourself not acting be aware of how your acting skills can help you. When you find yourself acting be amazed at how your other skills inform your acting. That way the mere act of living will feed your acting and your acting will enrich your life.'

Orion Lee – Oscar-nominated actor

After the Audition

Before we launch you head first into Week One, we want to ask you a question. How do you keep track of your meetings? If the answer is 'erm...' then this is for you.

We tend to focus a lot on preparing for auditions – learning lines, deciding what to wear, researching what the director's done before, etc. We go to the audition, do our thing and then say 'Well, I've done everything I can, it's in the lap of the gods now.' (And spend the next two weeks wondering whether or not to call your agent to see if there's any news).

But have you done all you can? For this audition maybe, but what about future ones? What if we told you the aftermath of the audition is almost as important as the preparation?

Well, we think it is. Not only does keeping a record of all your meetings allow you to track who you've met, when, where and make notes about the experience – it allows you to spot habits and patterns. Do particular songs tend to land you a musical gig? Have you got a lucky outfit? Does a certain casting director associate you with a specific genre?

Our friend Chris Clarkson is the absolute master of audition-logging and has clocked up a staggering 484 (and counting) castings on his log. After every meeting, he records anything and everything that could be potentially useful – from practicalities about travelling to the casting location, to any useful titbits of info about a casting director. Here's what he says:

'I keep a record of all the auditions I've had on a spreadsheet. It's really useful when I get a new audition to see if I've met the casting director or any of the people "in the room" before. For example, when I auditioned for a musical once the director and MD thought I was great but a bit too young for the role. I made sure I sang the same song next time we met, as they said it suited my voice well. Even niche info can be helpful: I was chatting to a casting director who mentioned who they supported football-wise. The next time I saw them I asked after their favourite team and their demeanour immediately softened. Another way it helps is when I get a casting to some obscure studio in the West End and I wonder if I've been there before. I can check and jog my memory of it (even adding stuff like "It's quicker to go round the back" or "There are NO TOILETS at this place"). Every little helps.'

The Challenge

Even if you haven't got any auditions on the horizon, you can still prepare your audition log so it's good to go when the next one lands. If spreadsheets aren't your jazz, how about a dedicated notebook or section on your phone? There are all kinds of weird and wonderful apps that make recording data fun so you could kill two birds with one pebble – discover a new app and improve your audition hit-rate.

Head to this link to download a template:

www.nickhernbooks.co.uk/jobbing-actor-templates

TOP TIP

Where are you carrying your tension right now? Jaw? Shoulder? Release that tension right now!

WELCOME TO A NEW WEEK!

Week Number: ❶   **Date w/c:**.........................

──────────── THIS WEEK'S GOALS ────────────

Career

....
....
....
....

Health and Wellness

....
....
....
....

Treats

....
....
....
....

Why are the above goals important to me?

....
....
....
....

What trip-ups might prevent me from hitting my goals?

....
....
....
....

Monday

....
....
....

Tuesday

....
....
....

Wednesday

....
....
....

Thursday

....
....
....

Friday

....
....
....

Saturday

....
....
....

Sunday

....
....
....

DAY 1 MONDAY

'I've had commercials off of the back of learning magic. I've done a telly just because I knew how to do skins (costume characters) work. The more skills you have in your Actor's Toolbox the more chance you have of being employed somewhere within this industry we love.'

Chris Clarkson – actor and presenter

—

Day/Date: ....

Daily Target: ....

How did today go?

....

....

....

....

....

What was one good thing that happened today?

....

....

....

———— TARGET PROGRESS ————

Did I complete any targets?

....

Did I identify any trip-ups?

....

Any additional targets?

....

DAY  TUESDAY

*'The days, weeks, months and sometimes years you are not officially
employed present an opportunity to create an actor's training
programme for yourself. I go to my personal actor's gym*
whenever I'm not employed.'*

Gethin Anthony – actor

—

Day/Date: ....

Daily Target: ....

How did today go?

....
....
....

What was one good thing that happened today?

....
....

TARGET PROGRESS

Did I complete any targets?

....

Did I identify any trip-ups?

....

Any additional targets?

....

* A metaphor for career-focused upskilling activities such as play-reading groups, acting classes, workshops or
self-tape practice. Every actor can create their own personalised version of the activities that help them grow
during periods of rest. In fact, this book is helping you do that right here, right now.

DAY 3 WEDNESDAY

'Start where you stand, and work with whatever tools you may have at your command, and better tools will be found as you go along.'

George Herbert – poet

Day/Date: ....

Daily Target: ....

How did today go?

....
....
....
....
....
....

What was one good thing that happened today?

....
....
....
....

TARGET PROGRESS

Did I complete any targets?

....

Did I identify any trip-ups?

....

Any additional targets?

....

—— MIDWEEK MOTIVATION & BOOSTER EXERCISE ——

Everyone's toolkits will contain different things, but there's a handful of core tools *every* actor must have, and one of those is self-taping. Here's an extract from an article from the lovely Rob Heaps (*Imposters, Good Girls, Dare Me*) who's landed most of his stellar roles through self-tapes alone.

> When I first started making self-tapes, I found the experience so stressful and traumatic that sometimes the only thing that kept me going was the hope that one day, after enough practice, I'd finally be able to knock out a tape as easily and quickly as a toasted cheese sandwich. I'm afraid self-tapes still stress me out but I have in fact figured out a way of taping that is easier and happier.
>
> Here is what I've learned – the hard way – over the last six years!
>
> The minute you receive a self-tape request, plan it. Here's how…
>
> Read the casting breakdown! Both for a) character notes and b) specific instructions – for instance, only send one take, use a mid-shot, American accent, etc. It's amazing how often people miss these and it will make you look very silly. If they've sent you the script, it's for a reason – read it for goodness' sake. It contains clues.
>
> Choose an appropriate taping partner. Try to tape with an actor, not just because they'll be better to read with, but also because they're more likely to understand and be generous with their time. Ideally someone you can return the favour to. Be careful about asking the same person too many times, even if they're brilliant to work with – especially if that person isn't auditioning much at the moment. Be sensitive.
>
> Fix a day and a time. Decide who you want to do it with and ask them well in advance, at least a day or two beforehand. Have back-ups.
>
> Get a decent tripod. I messed around for years with a tripod which had lost two of its screws and would topple over if it wasn't perfectly balanced. Why? Why did I do that? I really think it's worth spending more money

on good gear. What you get back in peace of mind and quality makes it more than worth it.

Get some basic soft box lights, or if you can afford it, some dimmable bicolour LED lights – they're a really good investment.

Watch the first take back immediately to check you're happy with the framing, lighting, eyeline, your hair. There is nothing worse than busting out some brilliant takes, heading home, then watching them back and realising that the camera was too close or that you had spinach in your teeth.

Now, here's a little challenge for you...

Self-(Tape) Improvement

We're all sailing at different speeds on the sea of self-tapes. You might have done one or two or you might have done two hundred. Whatever stage you're at, there's always an opportunity to improve.

- Write down three things you could do to improve your self-taping strategy. For example, creating a dedicated self-taping space with a clean backdrop, buying some decent lights or a tripod, inviting actor-chums to join a self-taping team.

- Pick one of these improvements and commit to doing it. If you can't do it today, diarise it for this week. Remember, it doesn't have to be a mammoth task. Start small, end mighty.

TOP TIP: EATING THE FROG

This is a top-notch technique for tackling those bloody awful jobs that are hanging over you. The ones that stalk you at night, creeping around your subconscious like a greedy joy-thief. Here's how. At the very beginning of your working day, decide to Eat the Frog. This is Bert & Butler (and Bill Gates) speak for tackling the worst job on your list FIRST. Once you've finished it, or at least made some headway, it'll make everything else on the list feel like jam on toast. Rinse and repeat the next day. And the next. And the... You get the idea.

DAY 5 FRIDAY

'You're helping us make sense of ourselves and others, of our world. You're carrying out a vital job. We're all relying on you. So prepare well, have faith, dig in and have fun delivering!'

Joss Agnew – Netflix director

Day/Date: ....

Daily Target: ....

How did today go?

....
....
....
....
....
....

What was one good thing that happened today?

....
....
....

TARGET PROGRESS

Did I complete any targets?

....

Did I identify any trip-ups?

....

Any additional targets?

....

DAY 6 SATURDAY

'Take classes. Keep working on and honing your craft with classes so you're sharp and ready when the time comes.'

Okezie Moro – actor

Day/Date: ....

Daily Target: ....

How did today go?

....
....
....
....
....
....

What was one good thing that happened today?

....
....
....
....

TARGET PROGRESS

Did I complete any targets?

....

Did I identify any trip-ups?

....

Any additional targets?

....

DAY  7 SUNDAY

'Never audition for practice … only ever practise to audition.
As a performer, you have only once chance to make a good
first impression. Make it count.'

Helen Lloyd – award-winning audiobook narrator

Day/Date: ....

Daily Target: ....

How did today go?

....
....
....
....
....
....

What was one good thing that happened today?

....
....
....

———————————— **TARGET PROGRESS** ————————————

Did I complete any targets?

....

Did I identify any trip-ups?

....

Any additional targets?

....

The C Word

Massive high five for smashing the first week!

Now, we want to take this opportunity to have a tête-à-tête with you about a core coaching principle: *consistency*.

There will be times over the next five weeks and beyond, when you get fed up and think 'Oh what is the point? It's not working, nothing's changed. How is spending ten minutes learning the ukulele going to land me a Disney+ gig?' Not only is this perfectly normal, it's actually a sign that you're engaging with the process. Change can be difficult because we can't see or feel it while it's happening. So what's the alternative? Give up? Nah. The crucial thing is to trust in the process, acknowledge that doubt and resistance are part of it and that consistency will be rewarded.

And actually, it's not really about learning the ukulele. It's about teaching yourself that you can make major changes over time by doing something minor on a regular basis. It's about learning how to be consistent, because when you do this, you become unstoppable.

The single best chance you can give yourself is to show up every single day, even if it's just to record your doubts in your journal. You can't reap the rewards without doing the work, without making the changes. Change takes time, persistence and grit – all of which you are capable of developing. In fact, you're doing it right now! So when you find yourself questioning the programme, here are four key things to remember:

- Stop focusing on short-term results. Life is not a ten-minute makeover show.

- Be in it for the process, not just the progress.

- Consistency is a muscle that needs to be exercised. Every. Single. Day.

- When you learn to be consistent, your life changes.
  It's the most valuable, transferable skill you'll ever acquire.

'Success isn't always about greatness. It's about consistency. Consistent hard work leads to success. Greatness will come.'

Dwayne Johnson – actor

WEEK 2
BRANDING

> *'The keys to brand success are self-definition, transparency,*
> *authenticity and accountability.'*
>
> Simon Mainwaring – branding expert and author

Week Two: Branding

Let's address the question on everyone's lips: What the hell is personal branding? Well, quite. If you're anything like we were, you might dismiss it as cringe-inducing showing off on social media. Yes, social media's part of it, but by no means all of it. And it doesn't have to be cringey. We asked branding and visual storytelling specialist Laura Evans from Nifty Fox Creative to pop it into a few words we can all relate to.

> *'Personal branding is your reputation; it's not what*
> *YOU say about YOU, but what OTHER PEOPLE say*
> *about you. So don't just tell people what you're about, show*
> *them in how you communicate, how you collaborate*
> *and how you show up authentically in the world.*
> *It's a bit like buying a soft drink – to pick up the can*
> *you need to be intrigued by the product, to keep*
> *drinking, you need to enjoy it.'*

So what does that mean for you as an actor? Well, at the risk of approaching broken-record territory, *you are your business*, and therefore need to consider how you present yourself. Yes but how? Another impeccable question... but before we get into the nitty-gritty of the *how*, we need to be very clear on the *who*.

The Who

We've compiled the following questionnaire with the help of branding expert and life coach Andrew Ryan. It's designed to unearth insights into who you are by identifying your key characteristics, values and vision for the future. This will then allow you to build a profile from a place of authenticity. Because that's what resonates. And by presenting your authentic self, you are enabling compatible collaborators to find you more easily and help you reach your full potential.

Who Am I?

What do you love about your job?

....

We know you've got loads of selling points, but what are your three *major* strengths?*

....

....

....

We can't all be perfect (thank goodness). Name three things you would change about yourself.

....

....

....

What is the one thing that people often get wrong about you?

....

What do you put that down to?

....

* If you are struggling to answer this, don't worry – this week's Midweek Motivation Exercise on page 67 will help!

Out of your current friends, which ones are most like you and why?

....

Which of your friends are most unlike you and why?

....

What are three things you often get complimented on?

....

....

....

Where can people find or interact with you (both in-person and online)?

....

....

What's your favourite TV show, film, play, website and social-media channel?

....

....

....

Who's the actor you are the most envious of/really admire?

....

Name a few people and/or companies you would *really* like to be involved with (directors, producers, theatre companies, casting directors and so on)

....

....

Finally... in five years, where would you love to be?

....

....

Hopefully the above exercise has started to get the right cogs turning, and is shedding some light on who you are, what you want and what you have to offer. If you'd like to go even deeper, head to this week's optional Midweek Motivation 'Secret Superpowers' on page 66, which explores the concept of finding and using your core strengths in more detail.

As well as encouraging clarity around what you want, we are trying to get you thinking objectively about yourself and how you show up in the world. Are you maximising your assets? Are you presenting the person you've just described in the best possible way? Does *what* you say match *how* you are saying it? Don't worry if you feel slightly overwhelmed at this stage or can't see the links, this is just the beginning.

You as a Product

Now we have unearthed some authentic foundations, it's time to start building on these from a branding perspective. As you work through the rest of this chapter, it is good to keep in the back of your mind that you are a product. Therefore if you are a product then casting directors, agents, directors and producers are your customers. Ask yourself the following questions:

- Why do you buy a particular brand of food or shoes?
- What is it about that brand that appeals to you?
- What have they captured so well that speaks to you and others?

As you move forwards, use any findings to inform your approach to your personal branding. If it appeals to you, it's more likely to appeal to the right audience or potential collaborators, with whom you have the most chance of forging a successful working relationship.

When creating and sustaining your brand, here are some things to consider…

- Are you presenting the person you just unearthed in the questionnaire?
- Are you being authentic? Don't pretend…people see through bullshit very quickly. Authenticity is the key.
- Are you sharing your story? In your own words? If people know your story, it builds up an element of trust, especially if you use your

authentic voice. Don't second-guess what people want you to say or how to sound. Be you. And then act like the person you promote yourself to be. It's all a delicious self-actualising loop.*

The How

So now we know who we are and what we're all about, how do we present that to the masses? Like it or not, the digital age is upon us and in order to 'show up in the world' we have to have some semblance of an online presence. If you're a tech dinosaur like Butler once was, don't despair, the following steps, tips and tricks will pave the way to building your brand into a perfectly presented package.

First things first, have you ever googled yourself? No, we don't blame you. Take a deep breath and do it now.

If you have an online presence ask yourself these questions, 'Is this the person I've just identified in the above exercise? Is it the person I want the world to see? If I was a casting director, would I invite me to audition?'

If you don't have an online presence, fret not. Think of this as a clean slate on which to make your mark. And don't panic – it's simpler than you think. There are plenty of methods available, a lot of which are free. At the risk of patronising you, we're going to go right back to basics...

Social Media

Below are the most popular social-media platforms, at time of writing:

Twitter
Instagram
Facebook
LinkedIn
TikTok
YouTube

You've probably heard of all of them, but if there are any you're not familiar with, get curious and investigate. You don't have to sign up to anything, you can just explore the site and get a feel for what's afoot. Your ultimate aim might be to have a profile on all

---

* Self-actualisation can be defined as the complete realisation of one's potential, and the full development of one's abilities and appreciation for life.

of them. But that may feel a bit overwhelming right now. We recommend focussing on the platform you're most comfortable with and building from there. If you know literally zero about any of them, here are some tips:

Twitter's particularly helpful in terms of connecting with fellow creatives, seeking advice and getting yourself out there. It suits people who enjoy expressing themselves through words, although posts with visual content get ten times more engagement.

Facebook isn't just for keeping in touch with friends and family any more. You can create a dedicated business page and connect more effectively with industry-focused groups, individuals and opportunities. It's easy to use and 60% of social-media users are on Facebook so it's a big old network.

Instagram is renowned as the best visual platform, so if you like expressing yourself through images and filmed content, then this is the platform for you. 62% of users log on every day, which keeps connection regular.

Facebook and Instagram are linked, so with the right settings in place, you can post content on both sites simultaneously. What a cracking time saver!

LinkedIn has an outdated reputation for being purely for the corporate world but is actually a great platform for making meaningful connections and applying for work across the creative sector.

TikTok isn't just for teenagers, contrary to popular belief! It's actually a hive of creativity involving a mix of music, lip sync videos, comedy, and micro-blog content. Admittedly it's difficult to grasp at first glance, but with a curious mind and a bit of time, it can be a great way to show the world what you can do.

YouTube may seem old hat, but is still up there as one of the best, most accessible online video and social-media platforms. Can't afford a website? Not on Spotlight yet? Then create your very own YouTube channel and upload your showreel/sample work for free. You can then email links directly to industry professionals in order to showcase your work. There's also scope to get really creative and have a bash at making content that may engage fellow industry folk whilst simultaneously raising your profile.

The positives of social media are aplenty. The immediacy, the outreach, the connectivity are all major plus points but there are, of course some pitfalls too. Whilst it is important to stay true to yourself and your beliefs; remember that everything you post is open to interpretation and commentary. Make sure you're representing yourself in the best possible way and try to avoid any knee-jerk posts or comments in the heat of the moment. Consider the potential impact of everything you post and remember that once something is out there, it can be difficult to retract.

It's also really important to make sure you're not over-using. If you sense you're getting too preoccupied with your social-media stats or are compulsively checking for updates and likes, try setting a daily engagement limit. Or experiment with a time-saving scheduling system like Hootsuite that allows you to post across multiple platforms at once. Because while social media's a reality, it's not Reality.

There's so much more to say on the topic of social media – we could write a whole book on it. Well, we couldn't but someone else could. This is really just an introduction to reduce any feelings of fear, get the creative juices flowing and inspire you to investigate what's out there.

Go forth and forage!

Personal Website

This is crucial if you don't have an agent or aren't on Spotlight yet.* A website is the numero uno way to promote yourself and have all of your information in one easy accessible place. A casting director would rather have a link to click than masses of attachments (CV, headshot, showreels, etc.) that will clog up their system.

'I'm not made of money you chumps! I can't afford a website!'

Actually, you can. There are some very affordable DIY website-building platforms out there. Have a quick google – you'll be surprised. You could have a fully-fledged website for the equivalent of a couple of trips to a snazzy coffee house every month. And remember it's all tax-deductible.

'Who do you think I am? Q from James Bond?'

No. You're you. That's the whole point. You don't have to be a tech-savvy coding expert to DIY-it. Sites like Squarespace and Wix have hundreds of brilliant templates you can personalise with step-by-step guides to steer you through the process. But if you've

* The Spotlight Link is the UK's most popular casting information service, used daily by industry professionals to send out their latest casting requirements to agents, and directly to performers.

still got sweaty palms just thinking about it, we have one word for you: outsource. We're not necessarily suggesting you go to a professional web designer – think outside the box. Are there friends or family members that could help? If money is tight, consider a skills exchange – what could you offer someone in return?

TOP TIP

Keep it simple. There's nothing worse than an overly complex website that's impossible to navigate. Think about websites you like using in everyday life. And ones you don't. What is it about them you like or dislike? Make lists.

Headshots

Yeah yeah, we know. Heard it all before. But there's a difference between knowing and doing. And this is such a crucial part of your package that we think it deserves its own section.

Finding a Photographer

It can be a very expensive part of your brand, so choose wisely. We know it can be an overwhelming process, so here are some key things to consider:

Don't go for a photographer just because they shoot famous faces. Go for the photographer whose style speaks to you.

When you look at their online gallery – are you drawn in? What's the overall tone of their work and would it suit your vibe as an actor? Do you want a studio or outdoor shoot? Does your agent have a preference? If you don't know, ask them.

Look at the headshots of actors you know personally. Do their headshots reflect who they are and the parts they could play? Or are they flattering to the point of rendering them unrecognisable?

Read the Google reviews!

Be brave and pick up the phone. If you're going to spend a couple of hours with someone, you need to know that you have some sort of connection, and that you're both clear about what you want and need from the shoot.

Choosing Your Headshot

Actors are notoriously terrible at choosing their own headshots. So *don't do it*. If you have an agent, trust in them. They are the ones 'selling' you on a daily basis. If you haven't got an agent, ask a *few* tell-it-like-it-is friends to select their top ten. Narrow it down from the ones that appeal to most of the group. Don't ask your followers on social media; that's too many opinions and it'll baffle the shit out of you. And they probably don't know you well enough.

You Need to Look Like You

We know it is so tempting to hide those little perceived imperfections, but they aren't imperfections, they are you in all of your glorious uniqueness. If a casting director brings you in, they're expecting you to resemble your headshot. If you don't, they're not going to high five you for it. So stay away from the airbrushing.

Let's Get ~~Physical~~ Practical!

These exercises are designed to kickstart your Personal Branding Plan of Action. It may seem like a heck of a lot for one week, and it is, so we recommend doing Step One this week, so you know what your theoretical plan is, then incorporate Step Two into your ongoing goals over the next few weeks and beyond.

Step One: In Theory

In this step we want you to create a theoretical plan of action to get this project to launch. Write down the series of steps you will need to take in order to achieve your end goal. It might look something like this:

1. Research what I already have in place and highlight what is missing.

2. Give myself a realistic deadline for launch of website and new social-media platforms, based on research.

3. Find a recommended website designer or enlist a tech-savvy pal.

4. Write a biog for use on website and make sure CV, headshots, showreel and voicereel are in good nick.

5. Launch website and revamped social-media profile.

6. Email casting directors, agents and directors on my HitList* with new information and link to website.

Step Two: In Practice

You have your theoretical plan of action so it's time to pad it out. In order to do this, you need to embark on a fact-finding mission by following these steps:

- Be a magpie. Research other actors and creatives, and nick the ideas that work. Be critical in your research – if you like or dislike something – ask yourself why. What is it about them and their image that you like? Do they have a top-notch website? What is it about their social media that lights you up? Was it easy to navigate? Could you find what you were looking for – details? showreel, etc.? Do they use a particular colour palette or image across all platforms so they are instantly recognisable?

- Work out what forms of social media suit you. Are you wordy (Twitter) or visual (Instagram)?

- Education. Education. Education. There are lots of free and low-cost workshops that cover all things social media and how to get the most out of it. Find one and book on.

- Source a website designer/photographer/friend in the branding-know. If money's tight, brainstorm everything you could offer in a skills swap. Remember that it doesn't have to be industry-related – it may be something like childcare or illustration or helping them decorate their house!

Step Three: Tagline

In this next step we want you to create your own personal tagline for use across your social-media channels – a Twitter bio or Insta profile. Fundamentally, it's a couple of short, punchy sentences that summarise who you are. If you've already got these, have a little check in with them – are they up to speed? Are they working well? Explore creatives you admire and see what they have written to give you some inspiration.

* More on this later.

We could give you some examples, but it's all totally subjective and is about what speaks to *you*. And we're here to springboard not spoon-feed!

This will probably feel a bit icky at first but push through the pain. Don't be afraid to blow your own trumpet. If you're feeling stuck, hit social media to see how other people have approached it.

We know it seems tiny, but attention to detail can make all the difference, so spend time researching, writing and rewriting. You can pack a hell of a punch with a handful of well-placed words.

'Life is not easy for any of us. But what of that? We must have perseverance and above all confidence in ourselves. We must believe that we are gifted for something and that this thing must be attained.'
Marie Curie – Polish-French physicist

WELCOME TO A NEW WEEK!

Week Number: 2

Date w/c: ....

―――――――――― THIS WEEK'S GOALS ――――――――――

Career

....
....
....
....

Health and Wellness

....
....
....
....

Treats

....
....
....
....

Why are the above goals important to me?

....
....
....
....

What trip-ups might prevent me from hitting my goals?

....
....
....
....

Monday

....
....
....

Tuesday

....
....
....

Wednesday

....
....
....

Thursday

....
....
....

Friday

....
....
....

Saturday

....
....
....

Sunday

....
....
....

DAY 1 MONDAY

'There has never been, in the 300,000 years of homosapien history, a human like you. You are unique on a cellular level. All the space dust, chance and probabilities that had to collide in that exact moment for you to come into being! Isn't that an amazing thought?'

Carrie Ekins – mentor and myofascial release therapist

—

Day/Date: ....

Daily Target: ....

How did today go?

....

....

....

....

....

What was one good thing that happened today?

....

....

....

TARGET PROGRESS

Did I complete any targets?

....

Did I identify any trip-ups?

....

Any additional targets?

....

DAY 2 TUESDAY

'You need a great reel. You need to figure out how to make a great reel for yourself. It doesn't have to be long, but putting a fantastic three minutes together is an important part of getting yourself ready to be taken seriously.'

Risa Braman Garcia – director, producer, casting director teacher and writer

Day/Date: ....

Daily Target: ....

How did today go?

....
....
....
....

What was one good thing that happened today?

....
....
....
....

TARGET PROGRESS

Did I complete any targets?

....

Did I identify any trip-ups?

....

Any additional targets?

....

DAY  3 WEDNESDAY

'If I focus on what I can do differently and better to everyone else, suddenly the competition goes away and it's more like you're in a competition with yourself, which is why figuring out your personal brand is just so powerful and is one of the biggest keys to having a successful long-lasting career.'

Kat Elizabeth – brand and messaging strategist

—

Day/Date: ....

Daily Target: ....

How did today go?

....
....
....
....

What was one good thing that happened today?

....
....
....

———— TARGET PROGRESS ————

Did I complete any targets?

....

Did I identify any trip-ups?

....

Any additional targets?

....

DAY 4 THURSDAY

——— MIDWEEK MOTIVATION & BOOSTER EXERCISE ———

We know it's been a busy week, so this is an optional exercise. It builds on the self-exploration you started doing in the initial questionnaire. If you're feeling overwhelmed or haven't got time, come back to it at a later stage.

Secret Superpowers

Believe it or not, you are jam-packed full of secret superpowers that can help you fly. We're talking metaphorically here, not caped crusaders and burning buildings. When harnessed, these superpowers can have an overwhelmingly positive impact on all areas of your life. However, most of us plod along, completely unaware of them. And if we don't know what they are, we can't use them. Which would be a shame.

What the Hell is a Superpower?

In a coaching context, superpowers are referred to as your core strengths. Think of them as your 'talent DNA' – the things that come easily to you. Simply put: stuff you're naturally good at or qualities you possess, like creativity, resilience, kindness, honesty, humour and so on. They can also include external resources available to you – e.g. friends with specific skills. Research tells us that using our core strengths on a daily basis leads to a much greater sense of wellbeing, and increased productivity/success. If we don't use them, we feel unhappy and unfulfilled.

Often we overlook our superpowers, because we take them for granted. We might assume that everyone is socially adept, or naturally analytical, or a dab hand at building IKEA furniture. But it's not true. Basically, we get so used to our own superpowers, that we don't maximise them and they become redundant.

This week, we're going to unearth these superpowers by taking another long, hard look at ourselves. It's not an exercise in self-flagellation – we do enough of that already – it's an uplifting, affirmative experience.

Let's crack on.

How to Find Your Core Strengths

Have a bash at answering these prompts to get the cogs whirring. Don't feel you have to do them all, just pick whichever ones appeal to you.

- What do I like most about myself?

- What am I proudest of?

- Can I think of a specific time when was I at my best, when life was good and I was flourishing?

- What do other people value most about me?

- What do I find effortless? What comes naturally to me?

TOP TIP

If you're struggling, ask yourself what others might say – a family member or a good friend; or try a strengths identification test online. We like this one because it's free, fun to do and makes you feel pretty darn good about yourself: www.viacharacter.org

Hopefully you've jotted down a few ideas? Good. Now highlight the five you feel are your strongest and write them below. These are your core strengths.

Consider these areas of your life: work, family/friends, personal growth, hobbies and relationships – and ask yourself the following questions:

1. In what areas of my life do I use my core strengths?

2. In what areas of my life are my core strengths lacking?

3. How can I use them more in these areas?

This exercise might also encourage reflection on any strengths you feel are lacking or perhaps even missing altogether. Rather than viewing this as a form of weakness, try to see it as an opportunity for positive growth, and ask yourself the following question:

Which core strengths do I feel I'm missing and would like to develop?

Now you are aware that there are gaps in your strengths set, you can take small but mighty steps towards developing them. Hoopla!

When you're goal-setting this week, have a think about how you can use your core strengths to achieve your goals. Now go forth and be fantastic.

DAY 5 FRIDAY

'Being cognitive of your brand and creating something that's authentic to you and your skill set is going to be a big difference maker in the success of your career.'

AMP Talent

Day/Date: ....

Daily Target: ....

How did today go?

....
....
....
....
....
....

What was one good thing that happened today?

....
....
....

TARGET PROGRESS

Did I complete any targets?

....

Did I identify any trip-ups?

....

Any additional targets?

....

'Your brand should encompass who you truly are — not a "cooler" version of you, but your authentic self.'

Indiana Kwong – actor and filmmaker

—

Day/Date: ....

Daily Target: ....

How did today go?

....
....
....
....
....
....

What was one good thing that happened today?

....
....
....
....

——— TARGET PROGRESS ———

Did I complete any targets?

....

Did I identify any trip-ups?

....

Any additional targets?

....

DAY 7 SUNDAY

'If you don't brand yourself now, you'll hate yourself later.'
Amy Joberman – HBO casting director

—

Day/Date: ....

Daily Target: ....

How did today go?

....
....
....
....
....
....
....
....

What was one good thing that happened today?

....
....
....
....

—————————— **TARGET PROGRESS** ——————————

Did I complete any targets?

....

Did I identify any trip-ups?

....

Any additional targets?

....

HOW'S YOUR MOTIVATION?

Are you sensing a lull in proceedings?
Feeling a bit lacklustre about the entire debacle?

Don't worry, it's just the two-week itch. Head back to page 47 and re-read the section on consistency.

Then revisit your 'Whys' and crack on.

WEEK 3
NETWORKING

Week Three: Networking

Love it or hate it, networking is part of your job. You might be the type of person who thrives on working a room, or you might be the kind of person who wants to hide under the buffet table snaffling scotch eggs. The good news is that there are different ways to approach networking these days, thanks to things like THE INTERNET. Yes, there will still be face-to-face schmoozing to be done, but the vast majority of networking can be done online. And, when you approach it with focus and integrity, it can be highly effective.

So, who's on your HitList?

We're talking contacts not contract killings. As an actor, much of your work will depend on a network of other people – casting directors, producers, agents, etc. It's your job to make yourself known to the key decision-makers in the industry – after all, how can they employ you if they don't know you exist or what you can do?

'If you don't ask, you don't get.'

This is a rule we live by, quite simply because it's true. Broadly speaking, humans aren't particularly good at asking for things, especially humans who happen to be actors. But all it takes is a bit of organisation, some fire in the belly, and tried and tested technique. All of which we can help you with.

You probably follow numerous influential folk on social media, but have you actually taken the time to find out who they are, what they do and whether they deserve a place on your HitList? Following someone on Twitter and giving them the occasional like is not the same as researching their career/upcoming projects and making a direct and tailored approach.

In this context, we are major advocates of quality over quantity. Sometimes we spread ourselves far and wide in order to reach out to people we think are important, but this scattergun technique is generally ineffective, exhausting and demoralising. So let's take this week to formulate a more structured approach to contacting your dream team of decision-makers, which will help establish a career of your design. Be the fisherman, not the fish!

Talking Tactics

You need to be tactical and organised about this, whether it's a mind-map, a spreadsheet or a dedicated HitList notebook. Find what works for you. Whatever method you opt for, we recommend starting with a good old-fashioned Brainsplurt (technical term).

How to Brainsplurt

It's incredibly straightforward. Get a massive piece of paper and some pens. Make lists, notes, bullet points or mind maps on the following:

- Existing Contacts

Who do you already know, personally or professionally, who's industry-related? Don't over-analyse their potential 'helpfulness' or the likelihood they'll cooperate or even respond for now; just get everyone down.

TOP TIP

Keep a notepad by the sofa (or wherever you watch stuff) so you can make notes as the credits roll. Make it a habit.

- Dream Projects

What sort of work inspires you? What have you seen that you'd love to have on your CV? Do you have a favoured genre or are you after variety? Research the production team on each project that you've enjoyed or admired. Who cast it? Who produced? Who directed? Take a look back at the 'Branding' section to remind yourself about your aspirations and check they're still aligned.

- Inspirational People

Actors

Which actors work do you respect and admire? Who's navigated the type of career you want? Research their journeys – where did they train? Who represents them? What were the early stages of their careers like? Can you find any interviews about them? What advice can they offer you?

Decision Makers

Which directors, agents, producers, casting directors do you want to collaborate with? You may have a healthy looking list after brainsplurting 'Dream Projects' but make sure you haven't missed any. THINK HARD and don't be frightened of aiming high. Shoot for the moon and all that. If you think you may have missed some, head to the Resources section on page 149 where you'll find a selection of websites jam-packed full of contacts.

Organisation Stations

You now need to compile all of the information above into an effective working document aka your HitList, as referenced earlier. Once you have completed it, you need to consider the following things before setting your targets:

- How many approaches do you want to make per day/week/month?
- Would you rather dedicate ten minutes a day to your HitList? Or are you more likely to stick to dedicating a whole day every month?

- Who gets priority? Consider numbering your contacts in terms of importance or relevance to your own goals. Perhaps some of them are time-sensitive – did you meet a director last week who needs a follow-up before the moment's passed?

- How are you going to keep your list current? The HitList system only works when you are diligent. You need to update it after every email, call, audition or chance meeting in a bar. Consider setting a weekly reminder on your phone or block out some time in your diary to check in with it regularly.

Time to set some targets!

Take a look at this week's Midweek Motivation for hot tips from industry professionals on how to make a stand-out approach, plus some super-inspiring success stories. If you think writing letters/emails is a waste of time, this section will blow your socks off. In a good way.

TOP TIP

What are your core values? The things that are truly meaningful to you? Make a list and ask yourself which ones you're neglecting right now...

WELCOME TO A NEW WEEK!

Week Number: 3   Date w/c: ....

───────────── THIS WEEK'S GOALS ─────────────

Career

....
....
....
....

Health and Wellness

....
....
....
....

Treats

....
....
....
....

Why are the above goals important to me?

....
....
....
....

What trip-ups might prevent me from hitting my goals?

....
....
....
....

Monday

....
....
....

Tuesday

....
....
....

Wednesday

....
....
....

Thursday

....
....
....

Friday

....
....
....

Saturday

....
....
....

Sunday

....
....
....

DAY 1 MONDAY

'You will often feel like the forgotten minority, but keep pushing, keep sticking that foot firmly in the door and not taking no for an answer.'

Philippa Griffiths – actor

Day/Date: ....

Daily Target: ....

How did today go?

....
....
....
....
....
....

What was one good thing that happened today?

....
....
....
....

——— TARGET PROGRESS ———

Did I complete any targets?

....

Did I identify any trip-ups?

....

Any additional targets?

....

DAY 2 TUESDAY

'Know where you want to go and make sure the right people know about it.'

Meredith Mahoney – CEO and designer

—

Day/Date: ....

Daily Target: ....

How did today go?

....

....

....

What was one good thing that happened today?

....

....

....

---------------------- TARGET PROGRESS ----------------------

Did I complete any targets?

....

Did I identify any trip-ups?

....

Any additional targets?

....

TOP TIP

When was the last time you had a totally social-media-free day?

DAY 3 WEDNESDAY

*'You have probably heard the saying 'it's not about what you know, but who you know.' Let me tell you that this rumour is false. It's not about who you know, **but who knows you**.'*

www.actinginlondon.co.uk

―――

Day/Date: ....

Daily Target: ....

How did today go?

....
....
....
....
....
....

What was one good thing that happened today?

....
....
....

―――――――――――――― TARGET PROGRESS ――――――――――――――

Did I complete any targets?

....

Did I identify any trip-ups?

....

Any additional targets?

....

—— **MIDWEEK MOTIVATION & BOOSTER EXERCISE** ——

Agents

Okey pokey. Let's talk about agents. Hands up who's spent a significant time with a group of fellow actors when the conversation HASN'T included questions like 'Who are you with?' or statements like 'My agent never puts me up for anything'? Yep. No one.

An agent can be the jewel in your networking crown, but as you'll see from Okezie's story below, it's not necessarily the be all and end all when it comes to securing work. If you're represented, this section will help you nurture and nourish the existing relationship with your agent, as well as offer general tips about how to approach the industry professionals on your HitList. If you're not represented, this section will help you work out who to approach – and how.

Remember that these approach tips apply to everyone on your HitList, so give it a read, even if you think you've got the networking nailed.

> *'Indifference is expensive. Hostility is unaffordable. Trust is priceless. It's all about relationships.'*
>
> Ted Rubin – professional keynote speaker

Let's do some myth-busting to begin with. Being an agent is not an easy job. For the vast majority, life is not spent at the Groucho Club wining and dining. The reality is that an agent's life is spent ten hours plus a day, sometimes seven days a week, at a desk, tied to a computer. An agent is a counsellor, business partner, life coach and friend. An actor wants to be in work; the agent wants you to be working. Never forget that. An agency needs commission to stay in business. If the commission isn't coming in, there's no money to pay the office rent or take casting directors to clients in shows – the whole operation grinds to a halt. An agency is a team and you are all paddling like mad to keep it moving forward.

Look at the bullet points below. Which one applies to you?

- I don't have an agent.

- I have an agent.

- I have an agent but I'm looking for a new agent.

- I've tried bloody everything and I can't get an agent.

Whichever category you fit into, securing, building and navigating the client/agent relationship takes determination and commitment. Make sure you read all the following sections as some advice crosses over.

I Don't Have an Agent

The majority of actors are unrepresented. So what can you do?

Research and build a database of potential agents. Be organised about it – knock out an Excel spreadsheet, or whichever method works for you. It will keep you accountable. Keep records of who, when and what the outcome was, so you have a systematic approach to making contact. Even with the best memory in the world it can get overwhelming.

If you are already at this stage, look back and read your emails. Be honest about the language, the approach. Simple things like a 'Dear Sir' when the agent is female, can show a lack of research and a blanket approach rather than a specific desire to be with them. Consider the quality and type of work their clients are securing. What would make you a good fit?

> *'Do not, under any circumstances, send me a biscuit.'*
> Philippa Howell – PHPM

Agents know why you are writing. Be succinct. Why are you writing? Make sure if you haven't anything to invite them to, that you have a link to your Spotlight page, website and that they have a showreel to view. They are not going to take you on if they haven't seen you in action. And for goodness sake, if you are going for the old-fashioned letter-writing approach: DO NOT put confetti in the envelope or a chocolate digestive telling the agent to relax and have a cuppa whilst they read your stuff. (All genuine approaches we've heard of). Spend more time looking at what you are sending, and the language you are using in your correspondence, to make you stand out.

I Have an Agent

Congratulations! For you, this week is all about taking stock. Get curious about your working relationship. How's it going? Are you happy? Is it working? What's great about the relationship? What's not so great? When was the last time you spoke to your agent? Do you feel comfortable checking in with them? If not, why? What could you say if you wanted to check in? If you don't know the protocol, what has prevented you asking them?

Remember it is a relationship. You might just want to say 'hello, how are you?' It's nice to ask how they are doing too. Or you might keep it business-focused and ask if you can do anything to support the submissions they have made or offer up some inside info you've come across. All relationships need to be nourished through communication, consideration and honesty – why should this one be any different?

Start by asking them how they would like you to keep in touch and how often is too annoying. If you don't ask the questions you will never know the answers.

Here's the marvellous agent Nicola Bolton with her perspective and top tips on How to Be A Model Client:

1. Be contactable at all times – or be able to pick up messages and respond as quickly as possible. This business is fast-paced and decisions are made quickly. If you need time out, just tell me.

2. Keep your Spotlight profile up to date with credits and skills.

3. Make sure your headshots are recent and if you have changed your appearance in any way, you will need new ones!

4. Learn material for a self-tape and submit it before the deadline. Follow the instructions that they have sent – this saves time.

5. Tell your agent if you are unavailable or going on holiday in advance. They may have been sorting a meeting for you and now you're going to Magaluf!

6. Work with your agent. They want you to achieve your goals and work. They are on your side.

7. Fail to prepare, prepare to fail. If you don't put the effort in, somebody else will.

8. If you have an audition or tape request, this means that the casting team think you could do the job! They are on your side.

9. Knowledge is power! Research and homework really do pay off.

10. Get a good knowledge of casting directors/directors in TV, film and theatre. You can find lots of information by watching the credits and looking online.

I Have an Agent But I'm Looking for a New One

Firstly, the grass isn't always greener. Be very sure that you have spoken with your agent and that the relationship isn't salvageable. Sometimes, it's a lack of communication (read the 'I have an agent' bit again). Most importantly, when you are contacting another agent for representation, don't slag off the agent you are with – it doesn't make you look good. Agents talk!! Similarly, tune in to the way your prospective agent talks about others within the industry, and ask yourself: 'Are our moral compasses aligned?'

I've Tried Bloody Everything and I Can't Get an Agent

If you haven't got an agent, don't despair. And don't wait until you have to try and get work. Here's why:

'When I was in my final year of drama school (LAMDA) I heard of a major Hollywood film casting in the UK. They were looking for young black men who could play soldiers. There were quite a few small roles available and they had seen a lot of my contemporaries… so I knew that even though I didn't have an agent yet they might still be open to meeting me as I was in my final year at drama school. I was bold enough to call the casting director and told them my situation and that I might be 'right' for the film. After sending over my headshot and CV they invited me for a meeting. After another audition a few months later I was offered a role. That film was Red Tails, produced by George Lucas. I got to work with Cuba Gooding Jr, Terence Howard and David Oyelowo and a young Michael B Jordan. All without having an agent.'

Okezie Morro – actor

DAY  FRIDAY

*'Have something to say about what you've been doing of late.
Even if you've not been working, what workshops or exercises
have you been doing?'*

Jermain Julian – director

—

Day/Date: ....

Daily Target: ....

How did today go?

....
....
....
....
....
....

What was one good thing that happened today?

....
....
....

——— TARGET PROGRESS ———

Did I complete any targets?

....

Did I identify any trip-ups?

....

Any additional targets?

....

DAY  SATURDAY

'Networking is not just about connecting people. It's about connecting people with people, people with ideas, and people with opportunities.'

Michele Jennae – creativity coach

Day/Date: ....

Daily Target: ....

How did today go?

....
....
....
....
....
....

What was one good thing that happened today?

....
....
....

——————— TARGET PROGRESS ———————

Did I complete any targets?

....

Did I identify any trip-ups?

....

Any additional targets?

....

DAY  SUNDAY

'If you're going to an industry event google or IMDB everyone and everything you can about the attendees. Learn as much as possible about the people you might meet with the intention of making a human connection.'

Nick Dunning – actor's high performance coach

Day/Date: ....

Daily Target: ....

How did today go?

....
....
....
....

What was one good thing that happened today?

....
....
....
....

TARGET PROGRESS

Did I complete any targets?

....

Did I identify any trip-ups?

....

Any additional targets?

....

Random Acts of Kindness

We know this is a slightly random place to pop this, but that's the whole point.

A random act of kindness can make a monumental difference to someone else's day. And to yours. Delicious dopamine floods your brain and body when you do something nice. Which is nice. So what are you waiting for? Let the nice times roll!

Here are some ideas to float your compassion canoe…

- Write something encouraging or positive on an online article or YouTube video you've enjoyed.
- Turn your computer off overnight – it helps the planet and your purse.
- Concoct a list of someone's best qualities and send it to them.
- Compliment a stranger.
- Let someone into a queue of traffic.
- Leave a book you've enjoyed on a park bench with a note inside to its new owner.
- Go litter-picking in your local park.
- Send a postcard to a relative or friend you haven't spoken to for a while.
- Make a cake or bake some bread for someone who'd really appreciate it.
- Do some voluntary work – see where you might be needed locally. Perhaps a soup kitchen, charity shop or animal sanctuary? Or if you're more outdoorsy, see if there's a park or heritage site nearby looking for rangers. If you're the literary type, your local library is a good starting point – there are some great organisations designed to inspire and aid creativity for vulnerable groups.

 **TOP TIP**

Having trouble doing a specific task? Set a timer for thirty minutes and see how much of it you can bang out in half an hour (it's just 2% of your day!).

WEEK 4
REJECTION

Week Four: Rejection

Hands up who likes rejection? No. Awful isn't it? Or is it? It's no secret that rejection is synonymous with an acting career. But knowing this doesn't stop the feelings of failure when a job doesn't land. But that's all rejection is – a 'feeling'. It's not a tangible thing. It doesn't actually change anything when you really think about it – just a future that doesn't even exist yet.

Like it or not, rejection is a huge part of an actor's life and that's never going to change. It's out of your control. But there is one thing you can change and control – and that is your reaction to it.

Here's how…

Acceptance

The sooner you *accept* the fact that being rejected is going to play a part in your life, the sooner you can embrace it and even use it to your advantage.

Do it now. Sit down somewhere quiet and make a conscious decision to accept rejection as part of the fabric of your chosen profession. Next time you experience a knock-back, acknowledge it for what it actually is: confirmation that you are an actor handling one of the more challenging areas of your job.

'What I would tell any young actor is: Hearing "no" doesn't mean "never".'
Antoinette Robertson – *Dear White People*

Understanding

There is a difference between blaming yourself for being rejected ('I'm not good enough') and understanding *why* you were rejected.

If you can, get feedback from your agent or the casting director – either about your audition, or who the part went to instead of you. You might learn something constructive about your audition technique that will win you bigger, better parts later down the line.

Or you could find out that you didn't get the job due to external factors beyond your control. Perhaps they opted for someone who looked more like the actors they'd already cast as parents/siblings. Perhaps the part was cut or the gender changed or the entire project got pulled. You just don't know. Even if you can't get feedback, don't automatically assume you didn't get the job because you weren't good enough.

Landing an acting job isn't just about talent. It's also about timing, luck and ultimately – business. These latter factors are beyond your control, so don't let them define your self-worth.

A Growth Mindset

All creatives have to learn how to handle rejection in order to succeed – take comfort from knowing you're part of this inspiring tribe, all growing collective thick skins in honour of pursuing their artistic ambitions. Author Stephen King used to collect rejection letters. In fact, he used to look forward to them, knowing that successful writers had to wade through hundreds of 'nos' before they started getting 'yeses'. Every time he received one, he took it as a sign he was one step closer to being a published author.

'By the time I was fourteen the nail in my wall would no longer support the weight of the rejection slips impaled upon it. I replaced the nail with a spike and went on writing.'

Stephen King – author

He's describing a growth mindset – i.e. using the setbacks to propel himself forward. You can do the same! When you get rejection, see it as a cue to kickstart something else – write to a casting director or revisit your toolbox and pick something to polish. Move on, safe in the knowledge you're a step closer to where you want to be.

They say 'no'. You say 'next'.

If you've always got something 'out there' bubbling away in the universe, you've got a reason to be hopeful. And where there's hope, there's – well, hope.

Gratitude

Maybe, just maybe, the universe has got your back and you didn't land the job for a reason.

Perhaps the project is destined to flop or there's a much more suitable job just around the corner. Perhaps you weren't truly right for the part and it would have hindered rather than helped your long-term career. Perhaps the universe is focusing on other aspects of your life – maybe you're destined to meet the love of your life in Lidl instead of touring with a show.

Experiment with this idea – look back at the overall dates of a job you didn't get and make a list of all the great things you would have missed out on if you'd got it. It might surprise you.

So next time you get a 'no', try to approach it philosophically, say thank you to the universe and look forward to the alternative opportunities it has in store.

Reframing Rejection: An Exercise

This is a cracker of an exercise, enabling you to take ownership of the way you respond to the inevitable rejections that will pepper your career path. Using the ideas below, you're going to design your very own Rejection Plan of Action, so you are equipped next time some chump turns you down. These are mere suggestions, so feel free to personalise them in any way you see fit.

- Take a specified length of time to really examine the feeling of rejection, accept it for what it is and decide to move on. Fifteen minutes should do it.

- Write a list of all the positives that came from the experience of being up for the job (e.g. I did a strong audition and they might use me for a different job; I met an up-and-coming director; I read a new play, etc.).

- Put another creative iron in the fire – email a director; add a few more candidates to your HitList.

- Reward yourself – you probably worked hard and did a cracking audition, which sometimes makes the rejection seem all the more unfair, so do something to acknowledge and then reward that success. You deserve it.

 THOUGHT OF THE DAY

What do the following people have in common?
Tom Hardy, Jada Pinkett Smith, Colin Farrell and Samuel L. Jackson.

Fame. Yes.
Sobriety. Also yes.
What's your relationship with alcohol like? Do you need to take a look at it?
Could it be hindering you in any way?

Now you've had a read of these suggestions, it's time to outline your personalised plan...

My Rejection Plan of Action

The next time I don't land a job, these are the exact steps I will take in order to move on in a positive and productive way:

....
....
....
....
....
....
....
....
....
....
....
....
....
....
....
....
....
....
....
....
....
....
....
....
....
....

TOP TIP

Have you been outside today? If not, whack those trainers out and go for a thirty-minute blast, whatever the weather.

WELCOME  TO A NEW WEEK!

Week Number: (4)   **Date w/c:** ....

———————————— THIS WEEK'S GOALS ————————————

Career

....
....
....
....

Health and Wellness

....
....
....
....

Treats

....
....
....
....

Why are the above goals important to me?

....
....
....
....

What trip-ups might prevent me from hitting my goals?

....
....
....
....

Monday

....

....

....

Tuesday

....

....

....

Wednesday

....

....

....

Thursday

....

....

....

Friday

....

....

....

Saturday

....

....

....

Sunday

....

....

....

DAY 1 MONDAY

'There were a lot of people I worked with in that same time period who gave up. But I prevailed and tenacity was a big part of the reason. I didn't give up. I didn't quit.'

Harrison Ford – actor

Day/Date: ....

Daily Target: ....

How did today go?

....
....
....
....
....
....

What was one good thing that happened today?

....
....
....

TARGET PROGRESS

Did I complete any targets?

....

Did I identify any trip-ups?

....

Any additional targets?

....

DAY 2 TUESDAY

'I kept showing up and I kept trying – I kept trying to push down the voice that was saying, "You're terrible. Someone's better than you. They're going to give the part to the other guy." And elevate the part of me that said, like, "You're worth it. You should be here."'

John Hamm – actor

Day/Date: ....

Daily Target: ....

How did today go?

....

....

....

....

What was one good thing that happened today?

....

....

....

....

TARGET PROGRESS

Did I complete any targets?

....

Did I identify any trip-ups?

....

Any additional targets?

....

DAY 3 WEDNESDAY

'They said, "You're Latina, you're very limited, the parts don't exist, you'll never make it as an actress here." In both scenarios, I thought, "What an interesting challenge. This is wrong. It must be changed." I had conviction because I was completely clear that this was what I had to do.'

Salma Hayek – actor

—

Day/Date: ....

Daily Target: ....

How did today go?

....
....
....
....

What was one good thing that happened today?

....
....
....
....

——— TARGET PROGRESS ———

Did I complete any targets?

....

Did I identify any trip-ups?

....

Any additional targets?

....

— MIDWEEK MOTIVATION & BOOSTER EXERCISE —

This week, we thought we'd treat you to snippets of an interview with none other than actor Eleanor Tomlinson of *Poldark*/*Outlaws*/general Hollywood-fame because she talks some serious sense when it comes to dealing with rejection.

- Personally I think it's extremely important for actors to be totally honest about their feelings in relation to casting opportunities, contact from agents and rejection. Far too often, actors are drawn into giving a polite but untrue response to any enquiry relating to their work status, instead of being able to feel that it is acceptable to reply "currently my professional life is shit".

- Rejection is never easy and I think there's an onus on casting directors to make the process less destructive by providing proper feedback. Every actor having put the work in to an audition/self-tape should at least be given an acknowledgment that the tape has been received. As the casting process progresses and an actor is invited to a further audition, screen test, chemistry test or the like, then they should be given constructive feedback on their work. This would go a long way in alleviating the torment and self-criticism that an actor can experience when rejected.

- I personally have learnt to not doubt myself or my ability when facing rejection and to not take it personally. It is worth noting though that this has taken me many years and some degree of success to achieve.

- When I'm going through a quiet time, I try to counteract the fact that I'm not working by concentrating on positive development. For example, I will make a point of watching the work of actors that inspire me and I will read books and plays that reignite my passion. My home environment and its energy also plays a crucial role. I believe that in order to have a positive mental attitude, you must enjoy the space you occupy. My home is my creative hub and being proactive creatively in that space is a good coping mechanism when acting work is not providing an artistic outlet.

- I think it's fair to say that rejection doesn't get easier, you just get used to it and grow a somewhat thicker skin. Some people may think that an established actor may fret less about future work prospects, but in actual fact the game is always changing and you have to keep on your toes. For example, the advent of social media and its power to create personalities means that competition for roles is becoming more and more popularity-based and so now actors are often expected to have an online persona and a sizeable following.

- If your heart is really in it, trust in your ability. Never stop watching and learning. Speak to creative people and find inspiration through that. But most of all, never give up. Some of the greatest actors were discovered in an unlikely way or later in life.

Now, here's this week's booster exercise. It's called The Wellness Toolkit. This is a bloody brilliant concept that can be revisited again and again. Once you've made it, it's always there, ready to supercharge you or simply scrape you off the floor.

What is a Wellness Toolkit?

In its simplest form, it's a technique designed to develop awareness of all the things you need in order to stay well. Sometimes it's difficult to recognise that we're struggling, let alone work out what to do about it. Having a Wellness Toolkit is a great way to prevent burn out, depression and anxiety. Here's how to go about it:

1. What are you like when you're feeling at your best? What characteristics do you display? How do you feel? How do other people know when you are feeling good about life?

2. What are the warning signs that indicate you're entering a 'slump' – i.e. a period of not feeling your best? How do you, or others in your life, know you've hit a bit of a wall? Perhaps you sleep more or less? What happens to your appetite? Are there certain activities you engage or disengage with? Perhaps you start to eat or drink more when a slump is afoot? Perhaps you stop communicating with your nearest and dearest? If you don't know, ask the people who really know and love you.

3. What has helped you out of the slump in the past? Think back to a low period in your life and make a note of all the things that helped you through it, for example: seeing specific friends, walking or spending time in nature, writing, cooking or listening to music, etc.

4. What do you know you need to do every single day to keep yourself feeling positive physically, mentally and emotionally? What are the non-negotiables in your life? Make a list of these things and pin it to the fridge/mirror/bedpost – somewhere prominent where you will see it. Get into the habit of checking them off everyday (it will help to get specific about when you need to do them – e.g. first thing/post work, etc.). You could even make a chart to ensure you're doing these crucial acts of self-love every single day. Soon enough they'll become second nature and you'll be nurturing yourself daily without even noticing! Here are some ideas from our own self-care routines to give you some ideas:

Journalling first thing, making a daily to-do list, stretching, yoga or walking, eating a wholesome but hearty breakfast, making the bed, avoiding social media for the first one or two hours of the day, having actual human contact – not just online, getting outside, avoid caffeine after 1 p.m. and technology two hours before bed…

TOP TIP

We adjust very quickly to our surroundings, so we tend to stop noticing new household additions after about three or four days. If you find you're forgetting to check your list daily, try moving it to a new location. Do this regularly.

5. Get creative. How can you collate everything you've learnt and keep that awareness going? Some people like to have a physical box containing wellness objects they can crack open when the black dog starts prowling. It might contain photos of friends, a favourite book or poem, or walking socks reminding you to get out in nature! Some people like to have a dedicated notebook or journal they can refer to, containing the answers to the above questions if things are going awry. It's also useful just to write it out sometimes. Writing is, after all, therapy as they say. Perhaps

you're a very visual person who responds to positive images and you fancy whipping up a wellness mood board as a painting or on Pinterest – go ahead!

 **TOP TIP**

Treat your body to a nice yawn and a stretch.
Just five minutes can perk your bod and brain right up.

DAY  FRIDAY

'The best way to guarantee a loss is to quit.'
Morgan Freeman – actor

—

Day/Date: ....

Daily Target: ....

How did today go?

....
....
....
....
....
....
....

What was one good thing that happened today?

....
....
....
....

——————— TARGET PROGRESS ———————

Did I complete any targets?

....

Did I identify any trip-ups?

....

Any additional targets?

....

DAY  SATURDAY

'I applied to drama school instead of university and got rejected from everyone. And Drama Centre London told me to be a children's TV presenter.'

Carey Mulligan – actor

Day/Date: ....

Daily Target: ....

How did today go?

....
....
....
....
....
....

What was one good thing that happened today?

....
....
....

TARGET PROGRESS

Did I complete any targets?

....

Did I identify any trip-ups?

....

Any additional targets?

....

DAY 7 SUNDAY

'I was in the middle of auditioning, and I was mid-sentence when the casting director said, "Listen, kid. You should not be an actress. You are not pretty enough. You should go back to wherever you came from and you should go to school. You don't have it."'

Winona Ryder – actor

—

Day/Date: ....

Daily Target: ....

How did today go?

....
....
....
....

What was one good thing that happened today?

....
....
....
....

————————— TARGET PROGRESS —————————

Did I complete any targets?

....

Did I identify any trip-ups?

....

Any additional targets?

....

HOW'S YOUR MOTIVATION?

Mojo gone missing?

Fret not, it's just the four-week itch. Change is an itchy business. But you know the drill: head back to page 47 and re-read the section on consistency. Then revisit your 'Whys?' and crack on.

WEEK 5
RESTING

Week Five: Resting

We're not talking about *resting* resting – the dreaded in-between-jobs/waiting-to-hear phase – but about proper R&R. You'll notice that this chapter is a touch shorter than usual because we like to practise what we preach.

Most actors don't have regular work schedules, so very few have regular rest schedules. Like many creatives, we are prone to 'The Freelancer Fear' and often live in a perpetual state of proactivity – either in terms of juggling resting jobs or pursuing activities we think may enhance our careers – unpaid projects, workshops, writing our own material, networking, etc.

Contracted employees have structured time-off because the traditional working week comes with in-built weekends. But as an actor, it's virtually impossible to instigate regular rest periods because your life could (and often does) change at any given moment. That is both the joy and the curse of the profession.

In addition to this, many actors are natural people-pleasers who find it difficult to say no, plus we're often superstitious about missing the mythical 'big break' if we turn something down. 'What if this director goes on to win a BAFTA? What if this unpaid fringe play transfers to the West End? What if I don't get another opportunity to act for the next six months?'

TOP TIP

What are you looking forward to? Have you got something fun lined up in the foreseeable future? If not, rectify this immediately!

It's this fear-fuelled 'scarcity mindset' (the notion that opportunities or resources are finite) that keeps our foot on the gas. And where does it take us? Burn-Out City.

So what can we do about it? There's no point saying 'just take a break', much better to go to the root of the problem…

The Battery Test

This very simple exercise will help you look at your life objectively and see what brings you energy and what depletes it. It goes like this:

- Write down the key elements of your daily life – technology, people, situations, events, habits, locations, environments, jobs, hobbies – you get the idea.

- Create two lists – 'Energisers' and 'Drains' and put each element into one of the categories, defined below.

  Drains

  What rinses the battery? What leaves you feeling exhausted, stressed or frustrated?

  Energisers

  What lights you up? What brings you joy? What makes you feel happy and fulfilled?

- Once you've finished, go through the Drains and highlight three things you could eliminate from your life.

- Look at your list of Energisers. Are there any missing? What energising people or pastimes do you wish played a bigger, more regular role in your everyday life? Add them to the list.

- Now, you've just created three lovely gaps by eliminating three Drains. How and when will you ensure you replace them with Energisers? For example, if you've realised that scrolling through Instagram first thing in the morning is a Drain, which Energiser could you replace it with? Yoga? Dog-walking? Meeting a chum for coffee?

- Commit to replacing three Drains with three Energisers. Be specific!

WELCOME TO A NEW WEEK!

Week Number: 5   **Date w/c:** ....

---------------- THIS WEEK'S GOALS ----------------

Career

....
....
....
....

Health and Wellness

....
....
....
....

Treats

....
....
....
....

Why are the above goals important to me?

....
....
....
....

What trip-ups might prevent me from hitting my goals?

....
....
....
....

Monday

....
....
....

Tuesday

....
....
....

Wednesday

....
....
....

Thursday

....
....
....

Friday

....
....
....

Saturday

....
....
....

Sunday

....
....
....

DAY 1 MONDAY

'There is virtue in work and there is virtue in rest. Use both and overlook neither.'

Alan Cohen – life coach and author

Day/Date: ....

Daily Target: ....

How did today go?

....

....

....

....

....

....

What was one good thing that happened today?

....

....

....

....

TARGET PROGRESS

Did I complete any targets?

....

Did I identify any trip-ups?

....

Any additional targets?

....

DAY  TUESDAY

'It takes courage to say yes to rest and play in a culture where exhaustion is seen as a status symbol.'

Brené Brown – professor and writer

―――

Day/Date: ....

Daily Target: ....

How did today go?

....
....
....

What was one good thing that happened today?

....
....

―――――――――――― **TARGET PROGRESS** ――――――――――――

Did I complete any targets?

....

Did I identify any trip-ups?

....

Any additional targets?

....

THOUGHT OF THE DAY

When was the last time you read a magazine? An actual magazine?
Head down to your local newsagent and have a peruse... you may be surprised.

DAY 3 WEDNESDAY

'Slow down and enjoy life. It's not only the scenery you miss by going too fast; you also miss the sense of where you are going and why.'

Eddie Cantor – performer

Day/Date: ....

Daily Target: ....

How did today go?

....

....

....

....

....

....

What was one good thing that happened today?

....

....

....

....

TARGET PROGRESS

Did I complete any targets?

....

Did I identify any trip-ups?

....

Any additional targets?

....

DAY 4 THURSDAY

*'We are like islands in the sea, separate on the surface
but connected in the deep.'*
William James – philosopher

—

We all need somebody. Simple as that. But we don't need *Everybody*…

This week's Midweek Motivation is going to allow you to take a closer look at who you spend time with and the impact they have on your life. Sounds stressful, but it's actually really interesting to take an objective view of your relationships. Sometimes we can find ourselves stuck in relationship ruts – spending time with the same people purely out of habit or a sense of duty, perhaps even at the cost of nurturing other, potentially more fulfilling relationships.

In a moment, we're going to invite you to do a Relationship Inventory. You may find everything is tickety-boo, in which case, great. Or you may discover an opportunity to spring clean and create space for people with whom you truly connect.

Surrounding yourself with 'your' people is integral to living a happy and fulfilled life. By 'your', we mean with those who bring out the best in you, who inspire and support you, and make you glad to be alive. It can be particularly important when making significant changes in our lives, as we may need to lean on people who have our best interests at heart.

So without further ado – let's have a bash:

The Relationship Inventory

- Make a list of the ten people you spend the most time with, outside of your immediate family.

- Put them in order 1 to 10 in terms of who you spend the most time with (1 = most, 10 = least).

- Give each person on the list a mark out of ten for the following:

  How much does this person champion me and/or my goals?
  How aligned are our values? i.e. the things we value most in life
  How much do we have in common in terms of hobbies, interests and activities?

- Now write down one word for each to describe how you feel when:

  You're about to see them.
  You have just parted company.

What did you learn? What surprised you? Is there anyone you are seeing out of duty or obligation? Are there other people in your life who deserve a place on this list? How could you make that happen?

This is probably obvious, but make sure you keep your thoughts and findings somewhere private. If the wrong eyes got a glimpse of a low star rating, it could have a damaging impact on your relationship – and we're in the business of making your life easier, not harder!

When you're goal-setting next week, think about how you can incorporate what you've learned from this exercise. It doesn't have to be a huge, life-changing action, like filing for divorce, it could be as simple as declining an invitation from someone you could do with seeing less of. Or calling someone you'd like to see more frequently.

Having a solid, reliable and inspiring social network or 'tribe' is integral to living joyfully. If you feel lacking in this department, here are some tips on how to tease out your tribe.

Find Your Fun

What activities or pastimes do you really enjoy? Perhaps you're a massive fan of fell-running but none of your friends are that keen to hit the hills. Or an avid quiz maestro without a team. Or a MasterChef in the making. If you branch out and do the things you love, you will inevitably find like-minded souls who share that passion.

Give It a Whirl

If you don't know where your true passions lie, have a go at anything and everything until you find them. Pottery classes, canyoning, comedy or cabaret nights? Even if you think it's not for you, there's no harm in testing the theory.

Don't Judge!

Often we lack the capacity to truly connect because we're too busy making surface judgements about people or activities. Ditch your preconceptions and go into every new social situation with an open mind. Look for the commonalities not the differences between yourself and others.

Make the First Move

If you can't find the group or meet up you're looking for, start it. There might be tons of hidden tribesters on your doorstep just waiting for someone to set up a Nepalese dance night or Knitters-what-natter group. And if you've already found the right team, but would like to forge a stronger bond, speak up and suggest a group outing or road trip.

'The more you embrace the weird crazy things about you,
the more you find your tribe.'

Jinkx Monsoon – performer and cabaret icon

───

TOP TIP

Take five minutes to visualise a part you'd love to play...
the universe is always listening.

DAY 5 FRIDAY

*'Rest and laughter are the most spiritual and subversive acts of all.
Laugh, rest, slow down.'*

Anne Lamott – novelist and activist

—

Day/Date: ....

Daily Target: ....

How did today go?

....
....
....
....
....
....

What was one good thing that happened today?

....
....
....
....

———— TARGET PROGRESS ————

Did I complete any targets?

....

Did I identify any trip-ups?

....

Any additional targets?

....

DAY 6 SATURDAY

'If you are tired, learn to rest, not to quit.'
@therandomvibez – motivational Twitter account

—

Day/Date: ....

Daily Target: ....

How did today go?

....
....
....
....
....
....
....

What was one good thing that happened today?

....
....
....
....

TARGET PROGRESS

Did I complete any targets?

....

Did I identify any trip-ups?

....

Any additional targets?

....

DAY 7 SUNDAY

'Take a rest; a field that has rested gives a beautiful crop.'

Ovid – Roman poet

—

Day/Date: ....

Daily Target: ....

How did today go?

....

....

....

....

....

....

....

What was one good thing that happened today?

....

....

....

....

———— TARGET PROGRESS ————

Did I complete any targets?

....

Did I identify any trip-ups?

....

Any additional targets?

....

WEEK 6
GOING ROGUE

'I've always found a cure for the blues is wandering into something unknown, and resting there, before coming back to whatever weight you were carrying.'

Diane Sawyer – American television broadcast journalist

Week Six: Going Rogue

A cting is a lot like dating; the more you try, the more desperate you become, the less people seem to want you. This chapter is all about taking a temporary break from acting in favour of flirting with other options and opportunities. It's time to play hard to get with acting and play the field of life instead. This may seem counterintuitive, given all you've covered over the last five weeks, but bear with us.

Going rogue, on more than one occasion, has led us to jobs that we never thought possible; to meeting people who have had an overwhelming impact on our personal and professional lives. Take this book for example – if we hadn't 'gone rogue', we would never have interviewed our lovely guest contributors, built a website or published this book. Bert would never have been crowned Business Captain and Butler would still be a tech dinosaur.

If you're concerned that diversifying means you've given up, WOAH THERE! Stop and tell Captain Negativo to get in the bin. You will always be an actor; nobody can ever take that away from you. It's in you, that is a given. Going rogue and exploring other talents might unleash even more extraordinary opportunities, ones that could end up strengthening your career or enhancing your existing talent.

THOUGHT OF THE DAY

When was the last time you treated yourself to some snazzy stationery?

Let's take Phoebe Waller-Bridge. She didn't go to RADA to train as a writer. She went to train as an actor. But she used her natural literary talent in conjunction with her acting skills and kaboom, look at what happened. First *Fleabag*, then *Killing Eve*. What next?

> *'Ah but that's one in a million. I can't write for toffee. She trained at RADA. My CV isn't as good.'*

We hear you. We can't all be Phoebe Waller-Bridge. Or Michaela Coel. Or Ricky Gervais. But there are other avenues! What are you good at? What do you genuinely enjoy? What will distract you enough from acting to simultaneously boost your confidence and creativity?

It doesn't have to be something directly connected with the industry either. Perhaps you're passionate about penguins or ping pong or punting? Mad about make-up or music or marmalade? Tantalised by travelling or tarantulas or twerking? Whatever it may be, you never know where it might lead. And while you're busy exploring, you're building confidence, giving yourself a new, positive focus and fulfilling some of the fundamental human needs that may have been neglected in favour of your fierce pursuit for filmic fame.

Yes, acting is the thing. But it's not the only thing.

Yes, you are an actor. But you're also a person. Sometimes, you need to reconnect with who that person is.

> *'I've learned that making a "living" is not the same as "making a life".'*
> Maya Angelou – author

How to Go Rogue

We've got some nice creative prompts for you to brainsplurt your way through. If you do this exercise properly, it should take about an hour. Don't rush through it half-arsed. Your future happiness deserves an hour of your present self's time. Think of it as a Happiness Deposit, rather than an annoying chore, and you'll be well away.

- Think back to your childhood – what did you used to love doing? What were you good at?

- Think forward to your deathbed (sorry) and write down all the things you wish you'd had a bash at.

- Think outside all of the boxes and write down EVERYTHING you'd love to have a go at if:

  a) Money wasn't an issue.

  b) You would definitely succeed.

  c) You weren't hindered by fear of any kind
     (including the judgement of others).

  d) Make a note of any people that cropped up when you
     read the above bit about judgement.

- Now write down every single last idea you've EVER had in terms of diversifying – a new business idea, a personal creative project, learning a new skill, going to a specific place – anything. Even if you can't see how it would help you right now, don't know how it would work or just seems utterly impossible.

- Can you see any reoccurring themes? Do your jottings reveal anything about your subconscious desires or potential blocks?

- Make one list of all your answers to the above, then read it aloud. Tune in to any internal reactions – which ideas spark the fire? Which ones make your heart do the fandango? Circle them.

- If you were only allowed to pick three to achieve in this lifetime, which would you choose?

- When you close your eyes, which of these three can you actually visualise yourself doing? To the point of completion?

- Let's go with this one. For the time being. You can always change your mind. Now, imagine for a moment that you were going to attempt this. What steps would you take theoretically? Try and be as detailed as possible.

- Now visualise what it would feel like, if you *actually* did this. If you achieved whatever it is. What impact would it have on your sense of self? In what ways would it positively impact your life?

- What would happen if you didn't do it?

- Look at the first step, see if you can break it down into even smaller steps. We're talking teeny weeny. Baby ones, if you will.

- Do the first baby step *right now*.

'The journey of a thousand miles begins with one step.'
Lao Tzu – ancient Chinese philosopher

THOUGHT OF THE DAY

How often do you say 'I haven't got time'? One hour is 4% of your day. Thirty minutes is 2% of your day. Fifteen minutes is 1% of your day. You've got time. Are you spending it wisely?

WELCOME TO A NEW WEEK!

Week Number: (6)　　　　　　　　**Date w/c:** ....

───────── **THIS WEEK'S GOALS** ─────────

Career

....
....
....
....

Health and Wellness

....
....
....
....

Treats

....
....
....
....

Why are the above goals important to me?

....
....
....
....

What trip-ups might prevent me from hitting my goals?

....
....
....
....

Monday

....
....
....

Tuesday

....
....
....

Wednesday

....
....
....

Thursday

....
....
....

Friday

....
....
....

Saturday

....
....
....

Sunday

....
....
....

DAY 1 MONDAY

'I couldn't just be an actor; the 'resting' was torture. I like to keep busy creatively so had to diversify. I saw a call-out, applied and from there began to write poetry then radio and eventually playwriting. I've found being on a development scheme an incredible tool to continue to learn and a way into the industry to being commissioned to create my own work.'

Charis McRoberts – actor and writer

Day/Date: ....

Daily Target: ....

How did today go?

....
....
....
....
....

What was one good thing that happened today?

....
....
....

TARGET PROGRESS

Did I complete any targets?

....

Did I identify any trip-ups?

....

Any additional targets?

....

DAY  TUESDAY

'Never be afraid to speak to other people who have done it and ask for their advice – there is a huge wealth of knowledge out there from people who are more than willing to share their learning and experience or signpost to others. Just ask.'

Hammerpuzzle Theatre Company

—

Day/Date: ....

Daily Target: ....

How did today go?

....
....
....
....
....

What was one good thing that happened today?

....
....
....

──────────── TARGET PROGRESS ────────────

Did I complete any targets?

....

Did I identify any trip-ups?

....

Any additional targets?

....

DAY 3 WEDNESDAY

'Be open-minded. The performance world is changing fast and new skills and understanding are required. Learn about the mediums that interest you and which are opening up. Do your research. Video Games, Mocap, Virtual Reality, Green screen, Volumetric capture, Augmented Reality.'

John Dower – co-founder of The MoCap Vaults

Day/Date: ....

Daily Target: ....

How did today go?

....
....
....
....
....

What was one good thing that happened today?

....
....
....

———————————— TARGET PROGRESS ————————————

Did I complete any targets?

....

Did I identify any trip-ups?

....

Any additional targets?

....

—— MIDWEEK MOTIVATION & BOOSTER EXERCISE ——

Earlier this week, you bravely took the first baby step towards Going Rogue. How did it make you feel? Empowered? Inspired? Or like the biggest imposter in Imposter City? Perhaps it was a combo of all three?

> *'It's not events that shape our lives, but our beliefs about them.'*
> Anthony Robbins – author

We're going to take a moment to talk about Limiting Beliefs which is a (semi)-technical term for all the naughty, negative things we say to ourselves that can kibosh motivation, productivity, self-esteem, success and overall wellbeing. Which is the antithesis of what we're gunning for.

In a nutshell, we are what we believe. Beliefs are the key to hell or happiness. We know that's a bold statement, but when you really think about it, it makes sense. Beliefs create emotions, which instigate action. Therefore, we're fundamentally driven by what we believe. We can't stop events happening, but we can choose how we interpret and act on them.

The good news is that we can actually tinker with our own internal belief systems, thanks to neuroplasticity, and create a mindset that will actively boost confidence, enhance productivity and have a whacking great impact on our chances of success.

First of all, we need to cultivate awareness around the negative internal belief systems that prevent us moving forwards. Because we've said before: Awareness is the catalyst for change! So, without further ado, it's time to....

Get to Know 'The Bastard'

We all have an inner critic – it's the internal voice that does a running commentary on all your flaws and the ways in which you already have, or will, 'fail'. Butler calls hers 'The Bastard'. It says things like this:

'You'll never get this job. You're too old/fat/short/ugly/unknown.'

'You look like a rabbit with myxomatosis.'

'You never see anything through, why would this be different?'

'Everyone will laugh at you when you fail. Again.'

Ring any bells? It's amazing how vile we can be to ourselves – I mean, would you put up with it from anyone else? Well then, don't take it from yourself either. The Bastard can be particularly active in the build up to doing something brave, like going rogue, so here are some techniques to tame them:

Top Tips for Banishing Your Bastard

- Christen it. Once it's got a name, you've actively separated it from you. Plus it makes it easier to bollock it.

- Make a list of all the claptrap it comes out with. What are their favourite phrases? What procrastination activities do they champion in order to curb your confidence/motivation? Do they call you names? Or make black-and-white statements about who you are and what you are/aren't capable of? These are your personal Limiting Beliefs.

- Read the list. Read it again. And again. Until you're familiar with all the catchphrases and techniques of your bastard. This creates the awareness we keep banging on about. What you're aware of you can control, what you're unaware of controls you.

- Substitute every Limiting Belief with a new Empowering Belief. These are positive statements about who you are and what you're capable of, such as: 'I'm a fantastic communicator' or 'I am brave, resilient and willing to try new things'. If you're struggling, go back to the Strengths exercise in Week One for inspiration.

- Spend some time getting to know your Bastard. Every time it pipes up with negative piffle, politely say 'Thank you for that contribution today, Mr Bastard/Eric the Terrible/Vivian, is there anything else you'd like to add?' Let them do a little monologue, then calmly counteract their argument with a barrage of Empowering Beliefs. The Bastard hates it when you talk like this because it makes them weak.

- Go back to your idea for Going Rogue. Record any instinctive Limiting Beliefs that crop up when you think about doing it. Exchange these for a series of Empowering Beliefs about yourself that would actively help you achieve this particular goal.

- Do baby step two…

'Always aim high, work hard, and care deeply about what you believe in. And, when you stumble, keep faith. And, when you're knocked down, get right back up and never listen to anyone who says you can't or shouldn't go on.'

Hillary Clinton – American politician

TOP TIP

Need a mood boost? Call someone who would really appreciate it.

DAY  FRIDAY

'You can't come out of school, whether it's LA or somewhere else, and expect to make a living acting. I know this sounds harsh, but you need to be ready to live the life of a non-paid actor, at least to begin with. And if you do get paid quickly, fantastic.'

Risa Braman Garcia – director and producer

Day/Date: ....

Daily Target: ....

How did today go?

....

....

....

....

....

What was one good thing that happened today?

....

....

....

―――――――――― **TARGET PROGRESS** ――――――――――

Did I complete any targets?

....

Did I identify any trip-ups?

....

Any additional targets?

....

DAY 6 SATURDAY

'Unless money is not an issue, there will be times you need to fall back on other skills to keep your income flowing. I've done a lot of non-acting work over the years and never with any intention of giving up my 'main' career. I've worked in bars, been a coach tour guide, managed theatre schools, taught drama, delivered parcels, mowed lawns… even set up my own theatre company. None of this should be seen as a 'failure'. Better by far to stay structured and proactive between jobs than fall into frustration (and debt!).'

Tom Roberts – actor

Day/Date: ....

Daily Target: ....

How did today go?

....
....
....

What was one good thing that happened today?

....
....

—————— TARGET PROGRESS ——————

Did I complete any targets?

....

Did I identify any trip-ups?

....

Any additional targets?

....

'I wasn't in California to party and go to clubs. I just kept myself immersed in the craft of acting so that when opportunity struck, I would be ready.'

Taraji P. Henson – American actor

—

Day/Date: ....

Daily Target: ....

How did today go?

....
....
....
....
....
....

What was one good thing that happened today?

....
....
....

—————————— **TARGET PROGRESS** ——————————

Did I complete any targets?

....

Did I identify any trip-ups?

....

Any additional targets?

....

WHAT NOW?

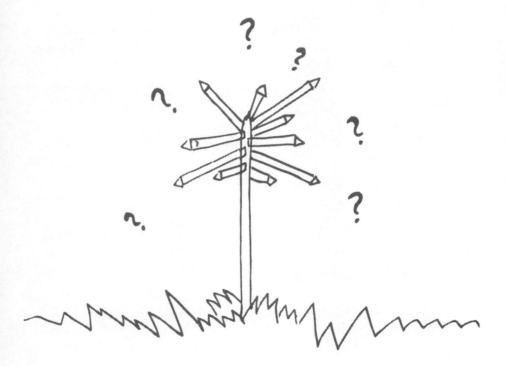

Beyond the Programme

So you've finished the six-week programme. Hoopla! Congratulations for sticking with it, digging deep and getting yourself to the finish line.

First things first, it's Smashing Reward Time! Go back to page 30 and have a little look at the promise you made yourself. If it's possible, do that thing now. If it's not, schedule a time to do it. You've earned it.

Second things second, if you've been fully engaged with the process, you will hopefully have some of the following things:

- A greater understanding of who you are, what you want and what you need.

- A deeper awareness of who/what inspires and supports you, and who/what does not.

- A regular reflective practice (aka journalling routine).

- Practical tools and techniques to draw upon in future.

- A sense of excitement and/or trepidation.

Yes, this is the end of this particular programme, but in reality, it is just the beginning. Before we launch you into the jungle like the tiger you are, we want you to take some time to reflect on the past six weeks because this is where the real learning happens.

'Reflection makes you realize that you already have a good base on which to build your next stage of development.'

Helyer, R. and Kay, J – authors/academics

So without further ado, we welcome you to The Reflection Section. Brew a pot, find a Jaffa Cake or three, and head to a quiet spot. The following exercise will take about half an hour.

The Reflection Section

Try to think critically about the questions below. Take some time before putting pen to paper to recollect the last six weeks and jot down any key happenings that spring to mind. It may help to flick back through each week, to make sure there's nothing you've missed. It's also useful to read each question a couple of times before you answer it. And when you do, be as specific and detailed as possible. Not only will this help solidify everything you've learnt, it will be a more effective reminder should you need to revisit your learnings later down the line.

- What elements of the process worked well for you?

- What elements worked less well?

- What tools, techniques or exercises will you take with you as you move forward?

- What goals or targets have you hit?

- What helped you hit these goals?

- What are your main obstacles or blockers in terms of achieving your goals (i.e. the people/places/things that continuously throw a spanner in your goal-setting works)?

- What have you learnt about yourself?

- In what ways has your attitude towards your career changed?

The Next Six Weeks and Beyond!

You've taken some time to reflect on the past six weeks, and now it's time to think about the upcoming weeks and months. This chapter is full of ideas about how you might decide to continue this process of change, arm yourself against the inevitable curveballs of life, and create space for ongoing reflection as you forge your path.

The Six-Month Plan

Describe your ideal next six months and the reasons behind these desires (aka your goals and their whys). It is important to focus on things you can control and then pair each one with a compelling reason as to why it's beneficial. For example:

Goal: Write or Perform a Short Piece at a One Act Play Festival

Why? To build confidence; create a sense of autonomy; expand my creative network; showcase my work to industry professionals; give me something to talk about in an audition; develop into a longer/larger project; for the sheer fun of it!

Order Your Goals in Terms of Importance

This is a quick way of working out your priorities. When things get hairy and you haven't got time to fit everything in, at least you know you are devoting what precious time you do have to the most important goal.

Create a System

We all need a system. How are you going to implement these goals? What routines, habits and tools do you need to employ to be successful? What does an average day look like?

How Will You Stick to the Plan When Things Get Tough?

What steps will you take to re-motivate yourself when you're fading? What tactics and tools could you use? Which friends or activities are boosters that will help you get back on track?

Why Do You Deserve This Improvement?

Okey pokey. This is a *biggie* as it challenges our brain's natural capacity to self-sabotage. Fill the space below with reasons why YOU ARE WORTH IT.

....

....

....

....

....

....

....

....

....

....

....

....

Staying on Track

'Knowledge is power.'

Wrong!

Knowledge is power *actioned*. We are very good at learning things, but tend to be less good at actually implementing whatever it is we have learnt. It looks something like this:

You have a leaky tap. It's driving you mad. You think to yourself one Saturday morning. 'I wonder how you fix a leaky tap. I know, I'll google it.' You flip open the laptop, scratch about online, watch a selection of tutorials until you come across one featuring a similar looking tap and think, 'Well, that looks pretty straightforward. I could probably manage it.' You close the laptop, have a cappuccino and that's the end of it. You know how to fix the tap, but that doesn't stop it from dripping. You need to actually implement the learning in order to get the tap fixed.

And it's the same with personal development. We read countless self-help books and listen to an array of podcasts, audiobooks, TED talks and think 'Oh yes, that makes sense' or 'I should probably give that a go' and promptly do nothing. So what do we do about it?

The Regular Review

Diarising a regular review of your goals is a brilliant way to hold yourself accountable and keep yourself on track. Decide *right now* when you are going to have these reviews – weekly, fortnightly, monthly? Be realistic about how much time you have and what you will actually stick to. Once you have decided, diarise the next three reviews and fully commit to them in the way you would to an important business meeting. You wouldn't let your agent/best friend/granny down – so don't let yourself down. Set reminders on your phone. Write it in capital letters in your diary. Or stick the date on the fridge. You could even recruit an accountability buddy* if that's viable. Just make sure you pick someone reliable and committed.

During these reviews, remember that you can always refer back to the coaching exercises in this programme. They can be a really useful comparison point, and are worth doing at different ages and stages of your life, so you can take stock of how far you've come and where you want to go next.

The Regular Review is an opportunity to reflect on progress and make any necessary adjustments. For the first one, just look back at your answers in the goal-setting section above and ask the following things:

- Am I on track?
- Why?/Why not?
- What adjustments do I need to make?
- What five things do I need to do to stay on track?
- What five things do I need NOT to do to stay on track?
- Have I got any new goals?
- What are they and why do I want them?
- When is my next review?

This may sound like a lot of effort, but in reality, it's half an hour every fortnight. That's half an episode of *Gogglebox*. We've all got that. But if writing is really not your

---

* Someone with similar goals and values, who will help you stay motivated and on track. (And vice versa, obviously!)

thing, there are other ways of keeping yourself in check with daily mental reflections or mindfulness practices. Have a go at these:

- Run through the next day's tasks/events in your head before going to sleep.

- Reflect on what happened during your day. What worked/didn't work/ how you can make changes.

- Chuck in some gratitude – what are you grateful for today? What has improved your life? It can be something as minuscule as a delicious sandwich or a nice smile from a fellow passenger on the bus.

- When you're having your morning cup of something, take a moment to think about the day ahead and say a little mental 'thank you' for whatever opportunities may lie ahead.

The Last Word

Thank you for taking a punt on this programme. We really hope you've found it an inspiring, empowering experience, and that you are looking at the future with a feeling of possibility and positivity.

You may be feeling a touch uncertain and apprehensive about going solo – that's natural – which is why we've created a 'Resources' section at the end of this book. You'll find a wealth of relevant websites, podcasts and books to support your next chapter. And remember we're never far away! Return to this programme whenever you need a boost, visit our website or follow us on social media for new exercises, industry interviews and hot coaching tips.

You'll find us @thejobbingactor on Instagram and Twitter.

Finally, if you've found *The Jobbing Actor* useful, please share the love and tell a fellow actor. Better still, gift them a copy as a treat! And never forget that…

'Today you are you!
That is truer than true!
There is no one alive who is you-er than you!'
Dr. Seuss – author and cartoonist

———

Great Big Massive Thank-yous...

Cor! What a lot of people we've got to high five for helping us bring this book to life. We'll do our best not to get soppy about it.

To everyone who contributed written or spoken material, gave us the time of day while we bandied ideas about, to our beloved fellow thesps and coaches, to all the people who rejected us, to all the people who didn't. To our parents, our pals, our readers and feeders, our agents and our editors.

With extra special thanks to:

Our brilliant beta readers: Andrew Ryan; Chris Clarkson; Denise Eaton; Stacey Sampson; Sophie Fisher.

All our cracking contributors: Joss Agnew; Gethin Anthony; Sarah Brigham; Nicola Bolton; Chris Clarkson; Philippa Cole; John Dower; Carrie Ekins; Laura Evans-Hill; Hammerpuzzle Theatre Company; Miranda Hart; Rob Heaps; Philippa Howell; Peter Hunt; Jermain Julian; Orion Lee; Helen Lloyd; Brendan McNamara; Charis McRoberts; Okezie Morro; Tom Roberts; Eleanor Tomlinson.

Our brilliant publishers at Nick Hern Books for taking a punt on a couple of chancers, with special thanks to Matt Applewhite for his encouragement, enthusiasm and editorial prowess.

Alan Frost – for his damn fine design skills and incessant cheerleading.

Katie Taylor – for her time, energy and making us write a business plan.

Joseph Willis – for his tech-wizardry and website-building prowess.

ScaleUp 360 – for their free business advice and support.

The writing of this book was made possible by the Sheffield Freelance Art and Culture Worker Fund created by Sheffield Culture Consortium, Sheffield Culture Collective, Sheffield City Council and the South Yorkshire Combined Mayoral Authority.

RESOURCES

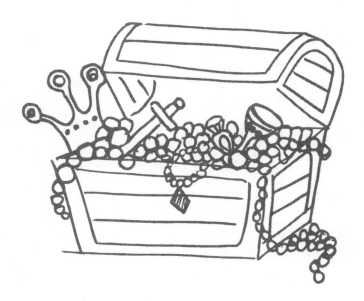

Resources

Here is a very nice starter collection of resources for you to explore. As always, we've added space for you to add your own findings as you continue to explore the adventure that is your own life!

Mental Health and Wellness

Websites

www.performersinmind.co.uk – A non-profit organisation working to campaign for mental-health action in the arts.

www.industryminds.co.uk – An award-winning and industry-leading mental-health charity for the creative arts.

www.bapam.org.uk – British Association for Performing Arts Medicine – Offers health and wellbeing services for those in the sector.

www.mind.org.uk – Mind – A charity devoted to providing advice and support for anyone experiencing a mental-health problem.

www.alustforlife.com – A movement for all things wellbeing.

www.actionforhappiness.org – A movement to make the world a happier place.

www.mindbodygreen.com – For daily wellness inspiration and news.

www.samaritans.org – A charity providing support for anyone struggling to cope.

www.wellbeinginthearts.org.uk – Mental-health and wellbeing support for individuals, productions and organisations in the arts.

www.oneyearnobeer.com – The leading website designed to help you take a positive empowering break from alcohol and reap the rewards, with 28, 90 and 365-day booze-free challenges.

Financial Support

www.actingforothers.co.uk/the-equity-charitable-trust – The Equity Charitable Trust – Helps all Equity members and professional performers and their dependants.

www.pipacampaign.com – Parents & Carers in Performing Arts – Promotes best practice employment and support for parents and carers in the performing arts sector.

www.actorschildren.org – Grants available to children of professional actors and offers advice and support.

www.trtf.com – The Royal Theatrical Fund – Provides support to those who have worked professionally in the entertainment industry for seven years or more, and are unable to work due to illness, injury or old age.

www.filmtvcharity.org.uk – The Film and TV Charity – Offers a wide range of financial, practical and emotional support to those within the industry.

www.actorsbenevolentfund.co.uk – The Actors' Benevolent Fund – Supports actors and stage managers experiencing hardship due to injury, illness or old age.

Podcasts

How to Fail – A brilliant podcast by Elizabeth Day devoted to reframing failure into a precursor for success, with an excellent array of guests. howtofail.podbean.com

Happy Place – Fearne Cotton interviews guests about life, loss and everything in between, exploring what happiness means to them. www.happyplaceofficial.co.uk/podcast

The Andy Ramage Podcast – The co-founder of One Year No Beer talks to inspiring guests on how they transformed their lives through believing in change. andyramage.com/podcasts

The Rich Roll Podcast – A deep dive into wellness with inspiring experts in health, fitness, nutrition, art, entertainment, entrepreneurship and spirituality. richroll.com/all-episodes

The Power Hour – Coach Adrienne Herbert talks to leading coaches, change-makers and innovators about their morning routines, daily habits and rules to live by. www.adrienne-london.com/podcast

Books

The Artist's Way by Julia Cameron

An Attitude for Acting by Andrew Tidmarsh and Tara Swart

Awaken the Giant Within by Tony Robbins

The Kindness Method by Shahroo Izadi

Letting Go by David R Hawkins

Man's Search for Meaning by Viktor E. Frankl

Mindfulness: A Practical Guide to Finding Peace in a Frantic World by Mark Williams and Danny Penman

Tiny Habits by BJ Fogg

Unf*ck Yourself by Gary John Bishop

Apps

Insight Timer – Guided meditations and mindfulness courses to create a calmer, happier mind. Plenty of free content.

Headspace – The forerunners of the mindfulness movement. Helps you create little pockets of peace throughout your day.

Calm – The number-one app for sleep and meditation designed to reduce stress and anxiety.

Career

Websites

www.equity.org.uk – Equity is the union for entertainment professionals in the UK and Ireland.

www.spotlight.com – Spotlight connects performers with roles in theatre, television and film productions. It's the go-to site for anyone working, or wanting to work, in the UK entertainment industry.

www.spotlight.com/contacts – A great place to search for collaborators or candidates for your HitList.

www.thecdg.co.uk – The Casting Directors Guild – A professional organisation of casting directors in the film, television, theatre and commercials communities in the UK and Ireland.

www.castingsociety.com – The Casting Society of America – The organisation for casting directors and associate casting directors in film, television, theatre and new media.

www.sagaftra.org – Screen Actors Guild – American Federation of TV and Radio Artists.

www.dialectsarchive.com – Free accent resource. Listen to numerous accents from around the world.

Podcasts

The VoiceOver Social – All the info you need in this lively podcast about the world of voiceover. www.thevosocial.com

The National Theatre Podcast – www.nationaltheatre.org.uk/content/nt-podcasts

Royal Court Playwrights Podcast – www.royalcourttheatre.com/podcasts/

SpotlightUK – www.spotlight.com/news-and-advice/interviews-podcasts/

The Honest Actors Podcast – play.acast.com/s/honestactors

Books

An Actor's Alphabet: An A to Z of Some Stuff I've Learnt and Some Stuff I'm Still Learning by Julie Hesmondhalgh

The Actors and Performers Yearbook – published annually

Advice from the Players by Laura Barnett

An Agent's Perspective by Natalie Payne

The Compact Guides – A series of books, published by Nick Hern Books, on key knowledge or skills for actors (e.g. getting into drama school, getting/working with an acting agent, learning your lines, making solo work, accents, etc.).

The Excellent Audition Guide by Andy Johnson

The Golden Rules of Acting and *More Golden Rules of Acting* by Andy Nyman

It's the Audition, Stupid! by Brendan McNamara

Surviving Actors Manual by Felicity Jackson and Lianne Robertson

The Working Actor: The Essential Guide to a Successful Career by Paul Clayton

Apps

The Accent Kit – Offers tools to learn new accents and build an accent library.

One Minute Voice WarmUp – A great pre-audition app to get your voice ready for action and keep it healthy.